The Fire 'n' Ice Cookbook

Mexican Food with a Bold New Attitude

By
Linda Matthie-Jacobs
&
Sheri Morrish

MJM Grande Enterprises Ltd.

The Fire 'n' Ice Cookbook

By
Linda Matthie-Jacobs & Sheri Morrish

Third Printing – July 2003

Canadian Cataloguing in Publication Data

Matthie-Jacobs, Linda, 1959-

    The fire 'n' ice cookbook

    Includes index.
    ISBN 1-895292-40-9

1. Cookery, Mexican.   I. Morrish, Sheri, 1966-
II. Title.

TX716.M6M37   1994   641.5972   C94-920173-1

Photography by:
Richard G. Warren
RGW Commercially Focused Photography, Red Deer, Alberta

Photo Design, Propping & Food Styling by:
Barry Weiss
Barry Weiss Intuitive Design, Calgary, Alberta

Cover and Page Design by:
Jennifer Nelson
Red Deer, Alberta

Dishes and Accessories Courtesy of:
Chintz & Company, Calgary, Alberta

Printed and Produced in Canada by:
Centax Books, a Division of PrintWest Communications Ltd.
Publishing Director: Margo Embury
1150 Eighth Avenue, Regina, Saskatchewan,
Canada S4R 1C9
(306) 525-2304   FAX: (306) 757-2439

Table of Contents

Recipes have been tested in U.S. Standard measurements. Common metric measurements are given as a convenience for those who are more familiar with metric. Recipes have not been tested in metric.

Preface

Through working together for several years in the oil and gas industry, we discovered we had many common interests, including a love of nutritious food, healthy lifestyles and cooking to entertain friends and family. A genuine enjoyment of Mexican food, and recognizing the trend towards Mexican and southwestern cuisine and design, inspired us to set off on an unfamiliar course to write our own cookbook. Nearly two years later, and after many repeated tastings and testings, we present to you our selection of recipes which encompass a variety of flavors in a wide range of menu categories. There are recipes to tantalize your tastes from morning to night, utilizing readily available ingredients and cooking methods to accommodate novice to experienced cooks.

While we don't claim to be food experts, we wanted to share our taste for the fire of peppers and the ice of cool beverages (we especially enjoyed "taste-driving" these recipes!). We both have full-time careers and this book is intended to be used by people as busy as we are who enjoy flavorful, nutritious food.

We've intentionally excluded salt from most recipes as we'd rather enhance flavor with the ingredients themselves. This is our own preference and shouldn't discourage you from adding salt to suit your own taste. In addition, although we didn't indicate in our ingredient listings, we used lower-fat dairy products and lean meats when we created the recipes for this cookbook. Whether you choose to cook with regular or lower-fat content products, you can be assured that the recipes will be delicious.

This book reflects our taste for "Mexican food with a bold new attitude" and we hope you enjoy it as much as we do!

Acknowledgements

We'd like to gratefully acknowledge the help and support of so many people that have been there for us through the development of this book:

- Jim and Bobby for their patience, love and support of our project, especially Jim for all his help running the business;

- Our parents for their eternal love and support;

- Richard Warren (RGW Commercially Focused Photography of Red Deer) for his incredible talent and perfectionism;

- Barry Weiss (Barry Weiss Intuitive Design of Calgary) for doing such a brilliant job of creating the concepts, designing our sets and making our food look so wonderful;

- Jennifer Nelson for her excellent cover and page designs, and for all her ideas and help while we were shooting the photographs in Red Deer;

- Chintz & Company of Calgary for generously allowing us to use their beautiful fabrics and props which were used in the photographs throughout the book;

- Carl and Elsie Matthie for the dried flowers, etc. used in the photographs.

- All of our friends and colleagues for their encouragement and support; and

- All those who enjoy our "Mexican food with a bold new attitude"!

Chili Facts

Chili peppers, ranging from sweet and mild to pungent and fiery, originated in the Western Hemisphere and were brought to Spain by Christopher Columbus. Today they are used around the world. There are more than 100 varieties native to Mexico and more than 200 varieties world wide. They are very rich in Vitamins A and C. Chilies vary from peppercorn size to 12 inches in length, and they vary in heat from 0 to 500,000 Scoville Units. Sweet bell peppers are rated 0, jalapeños are rated 5,000 and habañeros (Scotch bonnets) are rated from 100,000 to 300,000. Within each variety the heat can vary greatly, therefore, a taste test is recommended. The heat comes from capsaicin which is most concentrated in the veins or membranes, not the seeds as is popularly thought. To prevent burning your fingers, wear rubber gloves when handling hot chilies and do not touch your eyes or lips. To soothe a burning mouth, try bread, rice, corn, yogurt or milk drinks. Icy tequila-based drinks are also cooling.

Chilies are available fresh, dried, canned and pickled. If fresh chilies are unavailable, substitute canned. For hot chilies, substitute crushed dried chilies, hot pepper sauce or ground red pepper. Fresh chilies are green and ripen to yellow or red. They are seeded, deveined and used sliced or chopped. They may be roasted under a broiler or over a gas flame. When the skins are charred, put chilies in a pan and cover. Let them sweat for about 20 minutes and the skin will peel off easily.

Popular varieties of fresh chilies are: Anaheim or California, pale green and mild, about 4-6" in length; güero, wax, Hungarian or banana peppers, pale yellow or lime and mild to medium hot; poblano, ancho or pasilla, dark green, tapered and usually mild but occasionally hot, 3-4" long, very good for stuffing; jalapeño, grass green and medium-hot, about 2" long; serrano, bright green, tapered, hotter and smaller than jalapeños; habañero or Scotch bonnet, red, yellow, orange and greenish yellow, shaped like a top or tam-o'shanter, very hot to extremely hot.

Dried chilies need to be soaked in hot water for about 30 minutes before they are used. Save the liquid for sauces. Chop the soaked chilies and whirl in a blender or food processor with some of the liquid. Press the purée through a sieve to remove the tough skin.

Popular varieties of dried chilies are: ancho (dried poblano), brown, wide and a deep earthy, rich flavor, 3-4" long; arbol, bright red orange, brittle and hot, about 3" long and 1/2" wide; chipotle or moros (smoked, dried jalapeño), available canned in a spicy adobo marinade or dried and very hot, about 2" long, tapered and twisted.

Pepper Notes: Medical researchers at Ohio State University have proven that capsaicin reduces cholesterol levels significantly and is a factor in warding off strokes and heart attacks.

Hot peppers raise the body's metabolism rate for 20-25% longer than most other foods. If you are trying to lose weight, adding hot peppers to your diet may help.

Brunch Dishes

Huevos Ranchero

Ranch-Style Eggs — This superb combination of savory salsa and eggs makes a delicious breakfast or brunch dish.

2	tbsp.	vegetable oil	30	mL
1		medium sweet green pepper, chopped	1	
1		small onion, chopped	1	
1	cup	salsa	250	mL
1	cup	tomato sauce	250	mL
2	tbsp.	lime juice	30	mL
1	tsp.	Worcestershire sauce	5	mL
1/2	tsp.	chili powder	2	mL
6		8" (20 cm) flour tortillas	6	
2	tbsp.	butter or margarine	30	mL
12		eggs	12	
1/4	cup	shredded Monterey Jack cheese or Cheddar cheese	60	mL
		parsley or cilantro, for garnish		

In a medium saucepan, heat oil over medium-high heat. When hot, add green pepper and onion; sauté, stirring frequently, until onion is translucent. Add salsa, tomato sauce, lime juice, Worcestershire sauce and chili powder to vegetables. Bring to a boil over medium heat. Reduce heat to medium low; cover and simmer for 15 minutes, stirring occasionally.

Warm tortillas in oven or microwave*.

Melt butter in a large skillet over medium heat. Fry eggs, sunny side up, 4-6 at a time, until done as desired (scrambled or poached eggs can be substituted). Remove eggs from skillet and keep warm.

To serve: Place a tortilla on each serving plate and top with sauce and eggs. Sprinkle with cheese and garnish with parsley or cilantro. Serve immediately.

* To warm tortillas in a conventional oven, moisten a paper towel and place it in the bottom of a casserole. Place tortillas on top of paper towel and cover with a lid; bake at 250°F (120°C) for 15 minutes. To warm tortillas in a microwave, moisten 2 paper towels and lay 1 flat on a plate. Place tortillas on paper towel; cover with remaining paper towel and microwave on high for 30-45 seconds.

Serves 6.

Pictured on opposite page.

Huevos Ranchero, page 8
White Wine Sangría, page 17

Breakfast Burritos

1	tbsp.	butter or margarine	15	mL
1		medium onion, thinly sliced	1	
2	tbsp.	flour	30	mL
28	oz.	can stewed tomatoes	796	mL
1	tbsp.	butter or margarine	15	mL
2		small sweet green peppers, chopped	2	
2		medium onions, chopped	2	
2		garlic cloves, minced	2	
12		eggs	12	
1/4	cup	milk	60	mL
1/4	tsp.	black pepper	1	mL
6		10" (25 cm) flour tortillas	6	

To make the tomato sauce, in a small saucepan, melt 1 tbsp. (15 mL) butter over medium heat. Add sliced onion and cook until translucent; remove from heat. Stir in flour until smooth. Add tomatoes, cover, return to heat and bring to a boil. Simmer 3 minutes, or until slightly thickened; keep warm.

In a large skillet, melt 1 tbsp. (15 mL) butter over medium heat. Add green pepper, chopped onion, and garlic; cook, stirring frequently, until tender, about 5 minutes. Meanwhile, in a medium bowl, beat eggs with milk and pepper. Add to skillet with vegetables. Scramble eggs over low heat.

Warm tortillas (see Huevos Ranchero recipe, page 8, for method). Divide scrambled eggs evenly among tortillas, placing eggs in a row down the center. Fold burritos and place on serving plates (see illustration on page 12 for how to fold burritos). Cover burritos with tomato sauce.

Serves 6.

Note: If you prefer, or to save time, salsa can be substituted for tomato sauce.

Tortilla Quiche

1		10" (25 cm) flour tortilla	1	
1½	cups	shredded Monterey Jack cheese	375	mL
1	cup	shredded Cheddar cheese	250	mL
4	oz.	can chopped green chilies, drained	113	mL
3		eggs	3	
1	cup	sour cream	250	mL
½	tsp.	ground cumin	2	mL
¼	tsp.	cayenne pepper	1	mL
		salsa		

Preheat oven to 350°F (180°C). Press tortilla over the bottom and up the sides of a lightly greased 9" (23 cm) pie plate to form a shell. Sprinkle Monterey Jack cheese and half of Cheddar cheese over tortilla. Sprinkle chilies over cheese. Beat together eggs, sour cream, cumin and cayenne pepper. Pour over chilies and top with remaining Cheddar cheese. Sprinkle with cayenne pepper. Bake for 45 minutes and let set 10 minutes before cutting. Serve with salsa.

Serves 6.

To fold burritos:

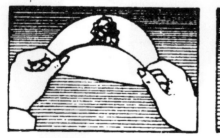 

Papas Y Chorizo

Mexican Potato Pancake

4		large potatoes	4	
1/2	lb.	chorizo sausage, see page 96	250	g
1		medium onion, finely chopped	1	
3		garlic cloves, minced	3	
4		small jalapeño peppers, finely chopped	4	
1	cup	sliced mushrooms	250	mL
1/2	tsp.	ground cumin	2	mL
		vegetable oil, for frying		
1	cup	shredded Cheddar cheese	250	mL
6		green onions, finely chopped	6	
1	tbsp.	finely chopped parsley	15	mL
		black pepper, to taste		
		salsa		

Peel potatoes and parboil for 10-15 minutes. Drain, rinse in cold water and set aside to cool.

Place chorizo, onions and garlic in a large skillet and cook over medium heat until browned. Add jalapeño peppers, mushrooms and cumin and sauté until tender. Remove from heat and set aside.

Generously oil a large skillet, at least 9" (23 cm) in diameter, and place over high heat. Meanwhile, shred potatoes on the large holes of a grater. When pan is hot, add half of the shredded potatoes and pat down with a spoon to pack evenly. Reduce heat to medium and cook potatoes, undisturbed, for about 10 minutes.

Sprinkle potatoes evenly with chorizo mixture. Sprinkle with cheese, green onions and parsley. Season to taste with pepper. Cover with remaining grated potatoes, making sure that potatoes are evenly distributed and all the cheese is covered. With a spatula flatten and even potatoes. Cook until golden brown, about 5 minutes.

Remove pan from heat and set on a flat work surface. Cover pan with a flat plate large enough to cover the surface completely. Holding plate and pan firmly, invert and remove pan so that potato cake is browned side up on plate. Wipe pan clean, oil again and reheat. Carefully slide potato cake, raw side down, into hot pan and cook until done over medium heat , about 15 minutes. Slide onto a heated serving plate and serve hot with salsa on the side.

Serves 6.

Peach Burritos

This dish also makes a delicious, light dessert.

2		large peaches, thinly sliced	2	
4		8" (20 cm) flour tortillas	4	
2	tbsp.	butter or margarine	30	mL
		cinnamon, to taste		
		brown sugar, to taste		

Arrange peach slices in a row near center of tortilla. Fold burrito.*
Repeat until all tortillas are filled.

Melt butter in a chafing dish or skillet. Place filled tortillas in the
dish and cook 4-5 minutes, until golden brown, turning once.
Remove from heat and sprinkle with cinnamon and brown sugar.

Serves 4.

* See instructions to fold burritos on page 12.

Chili Fruit Salad

This can be served alone as a
fruit salad or over ice cream for dessert.

3	tbsp.	cider vinegar	45	mL
2	tbsp.	sugar	30	mL
1/4	tsp.	crushed red pepper	1	mL
1	cup	cubed, seedless watermelon	250	mL
1	cup	cubed, fresh pineapple	250	mL
1	cup	sliced, fresh strawberries	250	mL

In a small saucepan, heat vinegar and sugar until sugar dissolves.
Stir in crushed red pepper and allow to cool.

Pour cooled sauce over fruit and stir. Chill until ready to serve.

Serves 4.

Beverages

Cantaloupe Fresco

1		cantaloupe, coarsely chopped	1	
1/2	cup	cold water	125	mL
2	tbsp.	lime juice	30	mL
1	tbsp.	liquid honey	15	mL
		ice, if desired		

Peel, seed and coarsely chop cantaloupe, and place in a blender. Add water, lime juice and sugar and purée until mixture is frothy and smooth. Divide between 2 tall glasses, adding ice if desired. Serve immediately.

Serves 2.

Note: This refreshing summer drink can also be a flavorful addition to a wine and soda base for a Cantaloupe Spritzer, or add white rum for a Cantaloupe Daiquiri.

Long Isla Iced Tea

6	oz.	white rum	170	mL
6	oz.	tequila	170	mL
6	oz.	Triple Sec	170	mL
6	oz.	vodka	170	mL
12 1/2	oz.	frozen limeade, thawed	355	mL
2 x 12 1/2	oz.	cans water	2 x 355	mL
		cola		
		lime twists, for garnish		

In a very large pitcher (approximately 64 oz. [2 L]), combine liquors with limeade and water. Add sufficient cola to make mixture the color of iced tea. Serve over ice in a tall glass with a lime twist for garnish.

Serves 8.

White Wine Sangría

Sangría takes its name from the color of the red wine. This is an inspired white wine version of the original.

½	cup	berry sugar	125	mL
½	cup	Grand Marnier	125	mL
½	cup	brandy	125	mL
2 x 26	oz.	bottles dry white wine	2 x 750	mL
68	oz.	bottle soda water	2	L
1		lemon, thinly sliced	1	
1		lime, thinly sliced	1	
1		orange, thinly sliced	1	
2	cups	halved, fresh strawberries	500	mL
		ice		

In a punch bowl, combine sugar, Grand Marnier, brandy and wine. Cover and refrigerate for at least 2 hours to chill. Just before serving, add soda water, fruit and ice cubes. Stir and serve.

Serves 12.

Pictured on page 9.

Variation: To make Red Wine Sangría, substitute red wine for white wine.

Branana Breeze

4	oz.	orange brandy	120	mL
4	oz.	banana liqueur	120	mL
4	oz.	lime juice	120	mL
		ice		

Fill a blender half full with ice cubes. Add liqueurs and juice; pulse chop until ice is crushed. Serve in chilled* gimlet glasses.

Serves 4.

* Place glasses in freezer for at least 30 minutes to chill. Remove from freezer just before serving.

Mazatlan Milkshake

2	oz.	tequila	60	mL
2	oz.	vodka	60	mL
4	oz.	Kahlúa	120	mL
3	cups	vanilla ice cream	750	mL

Blend all ingredients in a blender with crushed ice until smooth. Serve in chilled short glasses.

Serves 4.

Gazpacho Rapido (served in an ice bowl), page 64

Upside Down Margaritas

After a couple of these it won't be just the margaritas that are upside down!

26	oz.	bottle tequila	750	mL
26	oz.	bottle lime juice	750	mL

Put bartender's spouts on each bottle. Have the drinker sit or lie down and tilt his head back. Simultaneously, pour tequila and lime juice into the drinker's mouth.

Tequila Popper

1½	oz.	tequila	45	mL
½	oz.	7-Up	15	mL

Pour tequila into a shooter glass and top with 7-Up. Cover top of glass with the palm of your hand and bang on table. When 7-Up starts to fizz, drink as a shooter.

Serves 1.

Slow Mexican Screw

2	oz.	gin	60	mL
2	oz.	Southern Comfort	60	mL
2	oz.	Galliano	60	mL
2	oz.	tequila	60	mL
		orange juice		
		ice		

Fill 4 highball glasses with ice and pour ½ oz. (15 mL) of each liquor into each glass. Fill glass with orange juice and stir well.

Serves 4.

Tequila Sunrise

2	oz.	tequila	60	mL
¼	oz.	grenadine	7	mL
3	oz.	orange juice	90	mL
2	oz.	club soda	60	mL
		crushed ice		

Fill a tall glass with crushed ice. Add tequila and grenadine. Top with orange juice and club soda to fill glass. Stir.

Serves 1.

Cactus Cooler

5	oz.	tequila	150	mL
1	oz.	Triple Sec	30	mL
2	oz.	lime juice	60	mL
12	oz.	pineapple juice	340	mL

Blend all ingredients in a blender with crushed ice. Serve in a tall glass.

Serves 2.

Tequichis

5	oz.	tequila	150	mL
5	oz.	coconut milk	150	mL
5	oz.	pineapple juice	150	mL
		ice to fill blender		

Put all ingredients into a blender and blend for 1 minute. Serve in chilled short glasses.

Serves 4.

Daiquiris

12½	oz.	frozen limeade, thawed	355	mL
6	oz.	unsweetened lemon juice	170	mL
12½	oz.	white rum	355	mL
12½	oz.	water	355	mL
		ice to fill blender		

Mix all ingredients, except ice, in a large pitcher or juice container. Pour half of daiquiri mix into a blender, fill with ice and pulse chop until well blended. Pour into chilled gimlet glasses and serve. Repeat procedure for other half of daiquiri mix.

Serves 6.

Variations: Fresh or frozen strawberries, mango, peach, papaya, etc. may be substituted for the frozen limeade.

Margaritas

12½	oz.	frozen limeade, thawed	355	mL
6	oz.	tequila	170	mL
6	oz.	Triple Sec	170	mL
12½	oz.	water	355	mL
		ice to fill blender		

Put all ingredients into a blender and blend for 1 minute. Serve in chilled gimlet glasses. Glass rims may be salted or sugared if desired (dip top of glass in lemon juice and roll in salt or sugar).

Serves 6.

Variations: Fresh or frozen strawberries, mango, peach, papaya, etc. may be substituted for the frozen limeade.

Café Olé

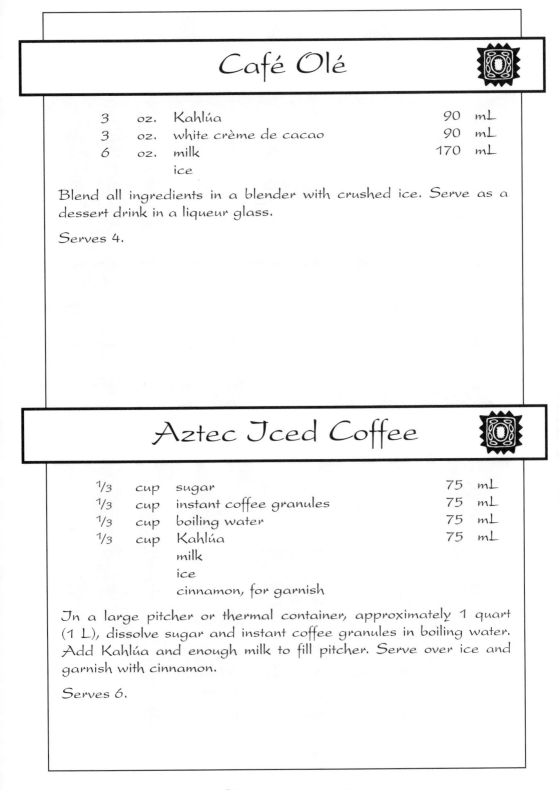

3	oz.	Kahlúa	90	mL
3	oz.	white crème de cacao	90	mL
6	oz.	milk	170	mL
		ice		

Blend all ingredients in a blender with crushed ice. Serve as a dessert drink in a liqueur glass.

Serves 4.

Aztec Iced Coffee

1/3	cup	sugar	75	mL
1/3	cup	instant coffee granules	75	mL
1/3	cup	boiling water	75	mL
1/3	cup	Kahlúa	75	mL
		milk		
		ice		
		cinnamon, for garnish		

In a large pitcher or thermal container, approximately 1 quart (1 L), dissolve sugar and instant coffee granules in boiling water. Add Kahlúa and enough milk to fill pitcher. Serve over ice and garnish with cinnamon.

Serves 6.

Mexican Coffee

1		large orange	1	
1/4	cup	sugar	60	mL
4	oz.	Kahlúa	125	mL
4	oz.	brandy	125	mL
4	cups	strong black coffee	1	L
1/2	cup	chocolate ice cream	125	mL
4	tbsp.	Kahlúa	60	mL
		cinnamon, for garnish		

Cut orange in half and press outer rims of brandy snifters into cut portion of fruit. Roll glass rims in sugar and heat glasses over flame to cook sugar onto rim.

Doing one glass at a time, add 1 oz. (30 mL) each of Kahlúa and brandy to glass, ignite and slowly roll liquid around glass for approximately 10 seconds.

Pour coffee into glass to fill. Top with a generous spoonful of chocolate ice cream.

Fill a tablespoon (15 mL) with Kahlúa and ignite. Slowly pour flaming Kahlúa over contents of glass and leave burning. Sprinkle cinnamon over top while flaming for fireworks effect.

Serves 4.

Breads

Corn and Flour Tortillas

1	cup	flour	250	mL
1/2	cup	cornmeal	125	mL
1 1/2	cups	cold water	375	mL
1		egg, well beaten	1	

Combine flour and cornmeal in a medium bowl. Add water and egg; beat until smooth.

Spoon 3 tbsp. (45 mL) batter onto a hot, ungreased griddle or crêpe pan and make a very thin 6" (15 cm) pancake. Turn tortilla when edges begin to brown and cook on the other side. Keep warm in a covered pan until ready to serve.

Makes 8-10 tortillas.

Note: Tortillas may be made ahead and frozen until ready to use. Place a layer of wax paper between tortillas to keep them separated.

Tortilla Crisps

4		6" (15 cm) flour tortillas	4	
4	oz.	can chopped green chilies, drained	114	mL
1/2	cup	shredded Cheddar cheese	125	mL
1/2		small sweet red pepper, finely chopped	1/2	

Preheat broiler. Place tortillas, 2 at a time, on an ungreased cookie sheet. Sprinkle top of tortillas with green chilies, Cheddar cheese and red pepper. Cut into quarters and broil until cheese is bubbling and edges of tortillas are browned. Remove from oven and serve.

Serves 4.

Pictured on page 55.

Guacamole Loaf

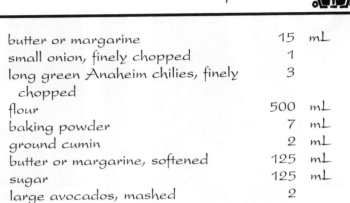

1	tbsp.	butter or margarine	15	mL
1		small onion, finely chopped	1	
3		long green Anaheim chilies, finely chopped	3	
2	cups	flour	500	mL
1½	tsp.	baking powder	7	mL
½	tsp.	ground cumin	2	mL
½	cup	butter or margarine, softened	125	mL
½	cup	sugar	125	mL
2		large avocados, mashed	2	
2		eggs, well beaten	2	

Preheat oven to 350°F (180°C).

In a small skillet, melt butter and sauté onion and Anaheim chilies until onion is translucent. Combine dry ingredients.

In a large bowl, cream together butter and sugar. Stir in avocado, eggs, onion and chilies. Add dry ingredients to avocado mixture and mix well.

Pour batter into a greased 5 x 9" (13 x 23 cm) loaf pan and bake for 55-60 minutes.

Makes 1 loaf.

Chorizo Bread

1/2	lb.	chorizo sausage, see page 96	250	g
3	cups	flour	750	mL
1	cup	shredded Cheddar cheese	250	mL
3		green onions, chopped	3	
3	tbsp.	brown sugar	45	mL
1 1/2	tbsp.	baking powder	22	mL
1/2	tsp.	ground cumin	2	mL
1/4	tsp.	baking soda	1	mL
8	oz.	cream cheese, softened	250	g
1	cup	milk	250	mL
2		eggs	2	
1/3	cup	butter or margarine, melted	75	mL

Preheat oven to 375°F (190°C).

Cook chorizo in a skillet over medium heat until brown and crisp. Remove from heat and drain thoroughly.

In a large bowl, stir together flour, cheese, green onions, sugar, baking powder, cumin and baking soda.

In another large bowl, beat cream cheese until smooth. Stir in milk. Add eggs, one at a time, beating well after each addition. Stir in melted butter and chorizo. Add to flour mixture and stir just until moistened.

Spoon batter into a greased 5 x 9" (13 x 23 cm) loaf pan. Bake until bread browns, about 55 minutes. Cool in pan on rack for 10-15 minutes, then turn out onto rack and allow to cool an additional 10-15 minutes before slicing to serve.

Makes 1 loaf.

Bandito Bread

1		loaf frozen bread dough, thawed	1	
1	cup	shredded Cheddar cheese	250	mL
1/2	lb.	cooked, drained chorizo sausage, see page 96	250	g
4	oz.	can chopped green chilies, drained	114	mL
1		egg, well beaten	1	
1	tbsp.	butter or margarine, melted	15	mL

Using greased fingers, press and stretch dough on a greased cookie sheet into a 6 x 12" (15 x 30 cm) rectangle. Set aside.

Prepare filling by combining cheese, chorizo, chilies and egg.

Spread filling on top of dough and roll lengthwise like a jelly-roll. Place on a greased cookie sheet, seam side down, cover and let rise at room temperature until doubled in size, about 2-4 hours.

Preheat oven to 375°F (190°C). Brush top of loaf with melted butter. Bake for 20 minutes.

Serves 8.

Panecillos

1		loaf frozen bread dough, thawed	1	
1/4	cup	butter or margarine, melted	60	mL
1		garlic clove, minced	1	
1/2	cup	grated Parmesan cheese	125	mL
1/4	tsp.	cayenne pepper	1	mL
1/4	tsp.	coarsely ground black pepper	1	mL
1/4	tsp.	crushed red pepper	1	mL

Cut bread dough into 8 equal parts.

Combine melted butter and garlic in a pie plate. Combine cheese and spices in another pie plate.

Roll each section of bread dough into a stick about 8" (20 cm) in length. Roll each bread stick in melted butter, then in cheese and spice mixture to coat thoroughly.

Place bread sticks on a greased cookie sheet and let rise in a warm place until doubled in size, about 45-60 minutes.

Bake in a preheated 400°F (200°C) oven for 10 minutes.

Makes 8 bread sticks.

Mexican Cheese Loaf

1		loaf French bread	1	
1/4	cup	butter or margarine, softened	60	mL
2		garlic cloves, minced	2	
14	oz.	can refried beans	398	mL
1/2	cup	salsa	125	mL
1	cup	shredded Cheddar cheese	250	mL
1	cup	shredded Monterey Jack cheese	250	mL

Slice bread in 1/2 lengthwise. Mix butter and garlic together and spread over both halves of bread.

Place on an ungreased cookie sheet and toast under broiler until just golden brown.

Remove from oven and spread refried beans on bread halves. Top with salsa and cheeses.

Place under broiler again until cheese is melted and bubbling. Remove from oven and cut into 8-12 pieces to serve.

Serves 8-12.

Jalapeño Corn Muffins

½	cup	flour	125	mL
1	tbsp.	baking powder	15	mL
1½	cups	cornmeal	375	mL
2		eggs, slightly beaten	2	
1	cup	sour cream	250	mL
1	cup	shredded Cheddar cheese	250	mL
1	cup	creamed corn	250	mL
¼	cup	finely chopped jalapeño peppers	60	mL
½	cup	butter or margarine, melted	125	mL

Preheat oven to 450°F (230°C).

Mix flour and baking powder together in a large mixing bowl. Add cornmeal, eggs, sour cream, cheese, corn, jalapeño peppers and melted butter. Mix until just moistened.

Bake in greased muffin tins for 15–20 minutes.

Makes about 12 large muffins.

Bacon-Jalapeño Muffins

1	cup	flour	250	mL
¾	cup	cornmeal	175	mL
⅓	cup	sugar	75	mL
1	tbsp.	baking powder	15	mL
1	cup	milk	250	mL
1		egg, beaten	1	
2	tbsp.	butter or margarine, melted	30	mL
4		strips bacon, cooked and crumbled	4	
4		jalapeño peppers, finely chopped	4	

Preheat oven to 425°F (220°C).

Stir dry ingredients together in a large bowl.

In a separate bowl combine milk, egg, butter, bacon and jalapeños. Add to dry ingredients and stir just until combined.

Spoon into muffin tins and bake for 15–20 minutes.

Makes 12–15 muffins.

Appetizers

Guacamole

3		ripe avocados	3	
1	tbsp.	lime juice	15	mL
1		large tomato, chopped	1	
1		large onion, chopped	1	
4		green onions, chopped	4	
1		sweet green pepper, chopped	1	
4		garlic cloves, minced	4	
4		small fresh hot chilies, finely chopped	4	
1/4	cup	chopped parsley or cilantro	60	mL
1	cup	sour cream	250	mL
1/8	tsp.	ground cumin	0.5	mL
1/4	tsp.	Tabasco sauce	1	mL

Mash avocados thoroughly with a fork. Add lime juice and mix well. Add remaining ingredients, mix well, cover and chill. Serve as an appetizer with tortilla chips or use as an ingredient in or a garnish for main dishes.

Makes about 3 cups (750 mL).

Note: Ripe avocados should be soft when squeezed and the outside skin almost black in color.

Variation: For a colorful and tasty appetizer, serve Guacamole-Stuffed Cherry Tomatoes. Using a sharp knife, cut cherry tomatoes in half crosswise, scoop out seeds and place upside down on a paper towel to drain for about 20 minutes.

Gently spoon guacamole into tomato halves. Sprinkle with bacon bits, fresh parsley or finely chopped green onion as garnish before serving.

Diablo Cheese Bowl, page 42

Seven-Layer Dip

8	oz.	cream cheese, softened	250	g
1/2	cup	sour cream	125	mL
1		garlic clove, minced	1	
1		large avocado, mashed	1	
1/2	tsp.	lime juice	2	mL
1		large tomato, chopped	1	
4	oz.	can chopped green chilies, drained	114	mL
1/2		sweet green pepper, chopped	1/2	
1/2		sweet red pepper, chopped	1/2	
4		green onions, chopped	4	
1 1/2	cups	salsa	375	mL
1/2	cup	shredded Cheddar cheese	125	mL
1/2	cup	shredded Monterey Jack cheese	125	mL

Combine cream cheese, sour cream and garlic, and spread in a 9" (23 cm) serving dish.

Combine avocado, lime juice, tomato and green chilies, and spread over first layer.

Sprinkle with green pepper, followed by red pepper and a layer of green onions. Spread salsa on top and sprinkle with cheeses.

Refrigerate several hours. Serve cold with tortilla chips and/or crackers.

Serves 8.

Salsa Cheese Dip

1	cup	shredded Cheddar cheese	250	mL
4	oz.	cream cheese, softened	125	g
1/4	cup	plain yogurt	60	mL
1		garlic clove, minced	1	
1/4	cup	salsa*	60	mL
2		green onions, finely chopped	2	
1	tsp.	finely chopped parsley	5	mL

Put cheeses, yogurt, garlic and half of salsa into food processor. Process until well blended.

Stir in the remaining salsa, green onions and parsley. Cover and refrigerate. Serve well chilled.

Garnish with cilantro leaves, parsley or sliced green onions and serve with assorted raw vegetables, crackers and/or tortilla chips.

Makes about 2 cups (500 mL).

* Choose mild, medium or hot salsa to suit your taste.

Creamy Pepper Dip

8	oz.	cream cheese, softened	250	g
1/2	cup	sour cream	125	mL
1/4	cup	shredded Cheddar cheese	60	mL
1/2		medium sweet red pepper, finely chopped	1/2	
1/2		medium sweet green pepper, finely chopped	1/2	
2		jalapeño peppers, finely chopped	2	
1	tsp.	crushed red pepper	5	mL
1	tsp.	ground cumin	5	mL

Blend cream cheese and sour cream until very smooth.

Stir in all other ingredients and chill for 1 hour before serving.

Serve with assorted raw vegetables, crackers and/or tortilla chips.

Makes about 3 cups (750 mL).

Mexican Roll-Ups

8	oz.	cream cheese, softened	250	g
4	oz.	can chopped green chilies, drained	114	mL
2		green onions, finely chopped	2	
1		garlic clove, minced	1	
8		6" (15 cm) flour tortillas	8	
		salsa		

Combine cream cheese, green chilies, green onions and garlic.

Divide cream cheese mixture evenly and spread on each tortilla. Roll and refrigerate for at least 2 hours.

Cut into 1" (2.5 cm) pieces and serve with salsa for dipping.

Serves 8.

Diablo Cheese Bowl

1	tbsp.	butter or margarine	15	mL
3		small jalapeño peppers, finely chopped	3	
1		medium onion, finely chopped	1	
3		garlic cloves, minced	3	
2	cups	milk	500	mL
2	tbsp.	butter or margarine	30	mL
3	tbsp.	flour	45	mL
2		eggs	2	
1/2	cup	salsa	125	mL
3/4	cup	shredded Cheddar cheese	175	mL
1/2	cup	shredded Swiss cheese	125	mL
1/2	tsp.	finely chopped dillweed	2	mL
1	tbsp.	finely chopped parsley	15	mL
3		green onions, finely chopped	3	
1		small, 8-10" (20-25 cm), round loaf of bread	1	
2	tbsp.	melted butter or margarine	30	mL
3		garlic cloves, minced	3	
		parsley, for garnish		

In a skillet over medium-high heat, melt 1 tbsp. (15 mL) butter and sauté peppers, onion, and garlic until onions are translucent, 3-4 minutes. In a blender, purée sautéed vegetables and milk.

In a saucepan over medium heat, blend together 2 tbsp. (30 mL) butter and flour, stirring constantly, for 2 minutes. Slowly add milk mixture and cook, whisking constantly, until mixture begins to thicken. Remove from heat and put 1 cup (250 mL) of mixture into blender. Add eggs to blender and blend until well mixed. Return saucepan to stove over medium heat and very slowly pour in egg mixture, whisking constantly. Continue whisking until mixture thickens. Add salsa, cheeses, dill, parsley and green onions, whisking constantly. When cheese is melted and thoroughly blended, reduce heat to low and keep warm while preparing bread bowl.

Preheat oven to 375°F (190°C). Cut top off bread, remove most of soft interior and tear it into bite-sized pieces for dipping later, leaving a 1" (2.5 cm) thick shell. Brush inside of loaf with 2 tbsp. (30 mL) melted butter and garlic. Bake, uncovered, until bread just begins to brown on inside, no more than 5 minutes. Remove from oven and place on a serving dish.

Diablo Cheese Bowl

Continued

Fill bread with warm cheese sauce. Let extra sauce spill over sides and onto plate. Garnish with parsley and serve immediately with previously torn bread pieces and sliced baguette.

Serves 6.

Pictured on page 37.

Chili Con Queso

1	tbsp.	butter or margarine	15	mL
1		medium onion, chopped	1	
14	oz.	can stewed tomatoes, undrained	398	mL
2 x 4	oz.	cans chopped green chilies, drained	2 x 114	mL
1	lb.	shredded Monterey Jack cheese	500	g
1/2	cup	milk	125	mL

Melt butter over medium heat in a medium skillet. Add onion, and cook until onion is translucent. Add tomatoes and green chilies. Reduce heat and simmer for 15 minutes, stirring occasionally.

Add cheese and stir constantly until melted. Add milk a little at a time, stirring constantly to keep from scorching, until mixture is smooth and very hot. Remove from heat and let stand 5 minutes to cool slightly.

Transfer to a fondue pot or chafing dish and keep warm. Serve with tortilla chips, raw vegetables and/or sliced baguette.

Serves 8.

Potato Skin Nachos

4		large baking potatoes	4	
1/2	tsp.	chili powder	2	mL
1	cup	salsa	250	mL
3/4	cup	shredded Monterey Jack cheese	175	mL
3/4	cup	shredded Cheddar cheese	175	mL
2		jalapeño peppers, finely chopped	2	
1		garlic clove, minced	1	
1	tbsp.	finely chopped parsley	15	mL

Scrub potatoes and bake in a 400°F (200°C) oven or microwave oven until cooked. Let potatoes cool until easy to handle.

Halve the potatoes lengthwise and scoop out pulp, leaving shells 1/8" (3 mm) thick. Halve each potato shell lengthwise, then halve each piece crosswise. Arrange potato skins, flesh side up, on an ungreased baking sheet. Sprinkle with chili powder and bake, uncovered, for 10 minutes, or until heated through.

Meanwhile, combine salsa, cheeses, pepper, garlic and parsley in a small bowl. Spoon mixture onto potato skins. With oven rack set 4" (10 cm) from heat, broil potato skins for 1-2 minutes, or until cheese melts.

Makes 32 nachos.

Note: Jalapeño peppers may be substituted with serrano chilies, habañero (Scotch bonnet) peppers, etc. depending on desired heat and/or market availability.

Piñata Puffs

2	cups	shredded Cheddar cheese	500	mL
1/2	cup	butter or margarine, softened	125	mL
1	cup	flour	250	mL
1/2	tsp.	cayenne pepper	2	mL
1/2	tsp.	paprika	2	mL
48		small green olives w/pimiento	48	

Preheat oven to 400°F (200°C).

Blend cheese with butter. Add flour, cayenne pepper and paprika; mix well. Mold 1 tsp. (15 mL) dough around each olive to completely cover.

On an ungreased cookie sheet, bake puffs for 15 minutes. Serve hot.

Makes 48 appetizers.

Note: These may be made ahead and refrigerated until ready to bake.

Savory Cheesecake

1	cup	finely crushed tortilla chips	250	mL
3	tbsp	butter or margarine, melted	45	mL
2 x 8	oz.	pkgs. cream cheese, softened	2 x 250	g
2		eggs	2	
1	cup	shredded Monterey Jack cheese	250	mL
4	oz.	can chopped green chilies, drained	114	mL
1	cup	salsa	250	mL
1		large sweet yellow or orange pepper, chopped	1	
4		green onions, chopped	4	
1		small tomato, chopped	1	
1/4	cup	sliced ripe olives	60	mL

Preheat oven to 325°F (160°C).

In a small bowl, stir together crushed chips and melted butter. Press into bottom of a greased 9" (23 cm) springform pan. Bake for 15 minutes.

Beat cream cheese and eggs in a large mixing bowl until well blended. Mix in cheese and chilies; spread evenly over crust. Bake 40 minutes, or until set in middle.

Remove from oven and spread salsa over cheesecake. Loosen cake from rim of pan and cool before removing. Chill. Top with remaining ingredients just before serving.

Serves 8.

Taco Tarts

1	lb.	ground beef	500	g
2		garlic cloves, minced	2	
1	tsp.	dried oregano	5	mL
1/2	tsp.	ground cumin	2	mL
1	tbsp.	chili powder	15	mL
1/4	tsp.	black pepper	1	mL
1	tsp.	crushed red pepper	5	mL
2	tbsp.	cold water	30	mL
1	cup	sour cream	250	mL
2	tbsp.	salsa	30	mL
1/4	cup	finely chopped ripe olives	60	mL
3/4	cup	coarsely crushed tortilla chips	175	mL
1/2	cup	shredded Cheddar cheese	125	mL
		sour cream		
		salsa		

Preheat oven to 375°F (190°C).

To make meat shells, combine ground beef, spices and cold water; mix well. Press meat mixture into the bottom and up the sides of small tart pans and set aside.

Combine sour cream, salsa, olives, tortilla chips and Cheddar cheese. Spoon filling into each shell, mounding slightly. Bake for approximately 30 minutes, or until meat shells are well browned.

Remove tarts from oven, remove from pans, and place on paper towel to absorb any excess grease. Place on serving dish and serve immediately with sour cream and salsa.

Makes 32 tarts.

Beef 'n' Bean Dip

1	lb.	ground beef	500	g
1		large onion, chopped	1	
2		garlic cloves, minced	2	
1	tsp.	dried oregano	5	mL
1/2	tsp.	ground cumin	2	mL
1	tbsp.	chili powder	15	mL
1	tsp.	crushed red pepper	5	mL
14	oz.	can refried beans	398	mL
4	oz.	can chopped green chilies, drained	114	mL
1	cup	shredded Monterey Jack cheese	250	mL
1	cup	salsa	250	mL
1	cup	sour cream	250	mL
4		green onions, chopped	4	
1		large tomato, chopped	1	

Preheat oven to 400°F (200°C).

In a large skillet, brown ground beef and onion; drain off excess liquid. Add spices and continue to cook for 5 minutes.

Spread refried beans in a 9 x 13" (23 x 33 cm) baking dish. Top with meat mixture. Sprinkle with green chilies, then top with cheese. Drizzle salsa over all and bake for 20 minutes.

Top with sour cream and garnish with green onions and tomato. Serve hot with tortilla chips.

Serves 8.

Beef Empanadas

		prepared pastry (enough for 2, 2-crust pies)		
1	lb.	ground beef	500	g
1		large onion, finely chopped	1	
4		garlic cloves, minced	4	
2	tsp.	cinnamon	10	mL
1/2	tsp.	ground cumin	2	mL
1/2	tsp.	ground coriander	2	mL
1/2	tsp.	ground cloves	2	mL
1	tbsp.	chili powder	15	mL
3	tbsp.	brown sugar	45	mL
1	tbsp.	vinegar	15	mL
1	tsp.	crushed red pepper	5	mL
1/2	cup	salsa	125	mL
		black pepper, to taste		

Prepare pie pastry. Refrigerate while preparing filling.

In a large skillet, brown ground beef, onion and garlic over medium heat until the meat is thoroughly cooked and onion is translucent. Drain off excess liquid. Stir in remaining ingredients and cook for 15 minutes over medium heat. Cool completely.

Preheat oven to 400°F (200°C).

Divide pastry into pie-sized portions, roll out on a lightly floured surface to 1/8" (3 mm) thickness, and cut out 4" (10 cm) rounds. Place a spoonful of filling on one half of each round and fold pastry over. Dip a fork in cold water and press outside edges of pastry together to enclose filling. Pierce top of each empanada with fork. Place on an ungreased cookie sheet 1" (2.5 cm) apart and bake for 12-15 minutes.

Note: The filling is already cooked so the empanadas only need to be baked until golden brown and heated through. These can be frozen and reheated. Serve warm with sour cream and/or salsa.

Makes approximately 8 dozen.

Mexican Egg Rolls

1	lb.	chorizo sausage, see page 96	500	g
1/2		medium onion, chopped	1/2	
1	cup	refried beans	250	mL
1	cup	shredded Monterey Jack cheese	250	mL
1/4	tsp.	ground cumin	1	mL
1/8	tsp.	cayenne pepper	0.5	mL
50		won-ton wrappers	50	
		vegetable oil		
		salsa		
		sour cream		

In a large skillet over medium-high heat, cook chorizo and onion until chorizo is crumbly and well cooked. Remove from heat and drain off excess liquid. Add beans, cheese, cumin and cayenne pepper. Stir until cheese is melted and filling is thoroughly combined. Let cool to room temperature.

Place a heaping teaspoon (10 mL) of filling on one corner of won-ton wrapper. Fold corner over filling to cover. Fold over left and right corners and brush sides and top with water. Roll, sealing corner.

Place finished won tons on a baking sheet. Fill and roll remaining won tons.

In a deep pan pour vegetable oil to 1" (2.5 cm) depth and heat to 350°F (180°C) or use a deep fryer. Fry 7 or 8 egg rolls at a time until golden brown, 2-3 minutes. Remove with a slotted metal spoon and drain on paper towels. Keep warm in a 200°F (100°C) oven until all egg rolls are cooked. Serve warm with salsa and sour cream.

Makes 50 Egg Rolls.

Note: Egg rolls can be made ahead and frozen. Reheat egg rolls in a 325°F (160°C) oven 10-15 minutes if thawed or 25-30 minutes if frozen. Do not reheat in microwave as they tend to go soggy.

Salads

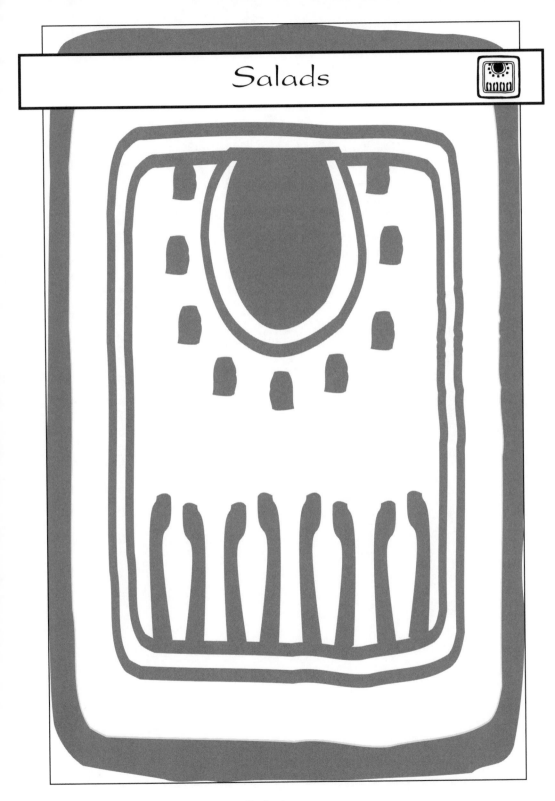

Salsa Salad

6		medium tomatoes, chopped	6	
3		medium avocados, peeled and diced	3	
1		medium English cucumber, diced	1	
1		medium red onion, chopped	1	
1/4	cup	olive oil	60	mL
2	tbsp.	lime juice	30	mL
1		jalapeño pepper, finely chopped	1	
1		garlic clove, minced	1	
1 1/2	tsp.	ground coriander	7	mL
1/4	tsp.	black pepper	1	mL
1		head of lettuce	1	

Gently stir together tomatoes, avocados, cucumber and red onion.

Combine olive oil, lime juice, jalapeño pepper, garlic, coriander and pepper by shaking in a covered container.

Pour dressing over salad and toss. Arrange lettuce cups on salad plates or create a bed of shredded lettuce and top with Salsa Salad.

Serves 6.

Tex-Mex Coleslaw

1/2	cup	mayonnaise	125	mL
1/4	tsp.	cayenne pepper	1	mL
1	tbsp.	sugar	15	mL
1	tbsp.	white vinegar	15	mL
1/2	tsp.	celery seed	2	mL
1/8	tsp.	black pepper	0.5	mL
1/2		head green cabbage, shredded	1/2	
1/2		head red cabbage, shredded	1/2	
4		jalapeño peppers, finely chopped	4	
1		Anaheim pepper, finely chopped	1	
1		small onion, chopped	1	
1	tbsp.	chopped parsley	15	mL

Stir together mayonnaise, cayenne pepper, sugar, vinegar, celery seed and pepper. Refrigerate for 2 hours to allow flavors to blend.

In a large bowl, toss green and red cabbage, jalapeño peppers, Anaheim pepper, onion and parsley. Add dressing and toss just before serving.

Serves 8.

Jalapeño Caviar

6		jalapeño peppers, finely chopped	6	
1/3	cup	olive oil	75	mL
1/4	cup	vinegar	60	mL
2		garlic cloves, minced	2	
1/4	tsp.	dry mustard	1	mL
		black pepper, to taste		
2 x 10	oz.	cans cooked black-eyed peas, drained and rinsed	2 x 284	mL
4		green onions, finely chopped	4	
1		celery stalk, finely chopped	1	

Combine jalapeño peppers, oil, vinegar, garlic, mustard and black pepper to make dressing.

In another bowl, stir together black-eyed peas, onions and celery. Pour dressing over, toss and refrigerate 2-3 hours or overnight.

Serves 6.

Pictured on opposite page.

Tortilla Crisps, page 28
Jalapeño Caviar, page 54
Sunshine Salad, page 57

Sunshine Salad

14	oz.	can pineapple chunks, drained, reserve juice	398	mL
1/4	cup	reserved pineapple juice	60	mL
2		large avocados, peeled and diced	2	
14	oz.	can whole kernel corn, drained	398	mL
1/4	cup	loosely packed fresh cilantro	60	mL
4		green onions, chopped	4	
1		large tomato, chopped	1	
2		large oranges, peeled and chopped	2	
1		garlic clove, minced	1	
1/4	tsp.	black pepper	1	mL

In a medium bowl, combine all ingredients. Refrigerate at least 1 hour before serving.

Serves 4.

Pictured on page 55.

Mexican Salad Dressing

This salad dressing adds a Mexican flavor to any pasta or garden salad.

1/4	cup	olive oil	60	mL
1/4	cup	salsa	60	mL
1/4	tsp.	black pepper	1	mL
1/8	tsp.	ground cumin	0.5	mL
1/8	tsp.	oregano	0.5	mL
1/8	tsp.	crushed red pepper	0.5	mL
2		garlic cloves, minced	2	

Put all ingredients in a container with a tight-fitting lid and shake vigorously until well combined. Store in refrigerator until ready to use.

Serves 6.

Ensalada De Naranja

5		large seedless oranges	5
1/2		large red onion, chopped	1/2
1/2		large jicama, chopped	1/2
1/4	cup	chopped fresh cilantro or parsley	60 mL
		crushed red pepper, to taste	

Peel oranges and thinly slice into rounds. Place half of the slices on a serving plate. Layer half the onion, jicama and cilantro on top of the orange slices. Repeat the orange, onion, jicama and cilantro layers. Season with crushed red pepper and refrigerate for at least 2 hours before serving.

Serves 6.

Note: Jicama is a turnip-shaped root vegetable with a brown skin. Peeled and sliced, it is eaten raw and has a crisp, refreshing, sweet flavor.

Cabo San Lucas Salad

2		jalapeño peppers, chopped	2	
1/4	cup	mayonnaise	60	mL
2	tbsp.	sour cream	30	mL
1	tbsp.	olive oil	15	mL
1	tbsp.	lime juice	15	mL
1		garlic clove, minced	1	
1/4	tsp.	sugar	1	mL
1/4	tsp.	ground cumin	1	mL
1/2	cup	diced jicama	125	mL
4		green onions, chopped	4	
		mixed salad greens — red leaf, butter, radicchio, torn in pieces		
1/4	cup	shelled sunflower seeds	60	mL

Combine first 8 ingredients in blender. Refrigerate 2-3 hours to allow flavors to blend.

Combine jicama, onions, and salad greens in a large salad bowl. Add dressing, toss and top with sunflower seeds just before serving.

Serves 6.

Chicken Jicama Salad

1/2	cup	mayonnaise	125	mL
1 1/2	tsp.	lime zest	7	mL
1		lime, juice of	1	
1	tbsp.	Worcestershire sauce	15	mL
1/2	tsp.	dried dillweed	2	mL
1/2	tsp.	cayenne pepper	2	mL
1/4	tsp.	dry mustard	1	mL
1	cup	sour cream	250	mL
2	tbsp.	tequila	30	mL
2		heads of butter lettuce	2	
2	cups	diced, cooked chicken	500	mL
1		medium jicama, julienned	1	
2		large avocados, peeled and sliced	2	
2		large tomatoes, cut into wedges	2	

To make dressing, whisk together mayonnaise, lime zest, lime juice, Worcestershire sauce, dillweed, cayenne pepper and dry mustard. When ingredients are well combined, mix in sour cream and tequila. Refrigerate for at least 3 hours to allow flavors to blend.

Tear lettuce into bite-sized pieces and place in a large salad bowl. Add chicken, jicama, avocado and tomato. Add dressing and toss just before serving.

Serves 6.

Pepper Salad

1		large sweet green pepper, thinly sliced	1
1		large sweet red pepper, thinly sliced	1
1		large sweet yellow pepper, thinly sliced	1
2		long Anaheim chilies, cut into rings	2
3		small jalapeño peppers, cut into rings	3
1		medium red onion, cut into rings	1
4	oz.	can chopped green chilies, drained	114 mL
1/2	cup	julienned cooked ham	125 mL
1/2	cup	julienned Gruyère or Swiss cheese	125 mL
		Pepper Salad Dressing, recipe below	

In a large bowl, toss together all salad ingredients except dressing. Chill while preparing Pepper Salad Dressing, which is shown below.

Pour dressing over salad and toss. Serve well chilled.

Serves 6.

Pepper Salad Dressing

2		garlic cloves, minced	2
1		small jalapeño pepper, chopped	1
1/3	cup	olive oil	75 mL
1/4	cup	cider vinegar	60 mL
1/8	tsp.	sugar	0.5 mL
1/4	tsp.	Italian seasoning	1 mL
1/4	tsp.	dried dillweed	1 mL
1/2	tsp.	Dijon mustard	2 mL

Purée all ingredients in a blender until creamy. Serve with Pepper Salad.

Serves 6.

Taco Salad

1½	lbs.	ground beef	750	g
1		large onion, chopped	1	
1		celery stalk, chopped	1	
1		large sweet green pepper, chopped	1	
3		garlic cloves, minced	3	
3	tbsp.	chili powder	45	mL
1	tbsp.	crushed red pepper	15	mL
14	oz.	can stewed tomatoes	398	mL
4	oz.	can chopped green chilies, drained	114	mL
2		green onions, chopped	2	
2	tbsp.	chili powder	30	mL
2-3	drops	Tabasco sauce	2-3	
½	cup	milk	125	mL
2	cups	shredded Cheddar cheese	500	mL
1		head of lettuce, shredded	1	
3		large tomatoes, chopped	3	
1	cup	black olives, sliced	250	mL
1½	cups	salsa	375	mL
		tortilla chips		

Brown ground beef in a large skillet over medium heat; drain off excess liquid. Add onion, celery, green pepper, garlic, chili powder and crushed red pepper, and simmer for 30 minutes. Keep warm.

Meanwhile, make chili con queso. Combine stewed tomatoes, green chilies, green onions, chili powder, Tabasco sauce and milk in a large saucepan over medium heat. Reduce heat and simmer for 20 minutes, then add cheese; stir constantly until melted. Keep warm.

Layer the salad ingredients in a deep, glass salad bowl or on individual serving plates in this order: lettuce, beef mixture, tomatoes, chili con queso, black olives, salsa, tortilla chips.

Serves 8.

Soups

Gazpacho Rapido

48	oz.	can tomato juice	1.36	L
2		garlic cloves, minced	2	
1		medium onion, quartered	1	
14	oz.	can tomato paste	398	mL
1		medium sweet green pepper, quartered	1	
1		large English cucumber, cut in 2" (5 cm) pieces	1	
1	tsp.	black pepper	5	mL
3	tbsp.	olive oil	45	mL
3	tbsp.	red wine vinegar	45	mL
1	cup	salsa	250	mL
		sour cream, for garnish		
		chopped parsley, for garnish		

Pour ⅓ of tomato juice into a blender. Add garlic and onion and blend until vegetables are puréed. Pour mixture into a large bowl. Add another ⅓ of tomato juice, tomato paste and green pepper to blender and blend until green pepper is puréed. Add to mixture in bowl. Pour remaining ⅓ of tomato juice into blender. Add unpeeled cucumber, pepper, oil and vinegar and blend. Add to mixture in bowl. Add salsa and stir to combine. Gazpacho should be made 24 hours ahead and refrigerated to allow flavors to blend.

To serve, ladle soup into serving bowls, put a dollop of sour cream in each, and swirl with a knife to create a marbled effect. Sprinkle with chopped parsley.

For entertaining and as a really dramatic serving idea, serve the gazpacho to your guests in a block of ice! Take a large container (a square or rectangular tub works perfectly) and fill ¾ full with water. Float a bowl the size required for the soup on the surface, then place sufficient weight (it doesn't matter what, just as long as it weighs enough to sink the bowl to its rim and can be lifted out when the ice is formed). Secure floating bowl with masking tape to the outside tub to keep centered. Freeze ice block until ready to serve. When ready to serve, place ice block in a high-sided serving dish to hold the water when the ice begins to melt, remove center bowl (you may have to loosen it with boiling water), pour in soup, garnish and present to your guests.

Serves 8.

Pictured on page 19.

Sopa De Aguacate

Avocado Soup

4	cups	chicken broth	1	L
1		large onion, chopped	1	
2		small jalapeño peppers, finely chopped	2	
2		garlic cloves, minced	2	
1/2	cup	cream sherry	125	mL
3		large ripe avocados	3	
1	cup	whipping cream	250	mL
		black pepper, to taste		
		cayenne pepper, to taste		
		chopped parsley, for garnish		

In a large saucepan, bring broth, onion, jalapeños and garlic to a boil. Reduce heat and simmer for 15-20 minutes.

Cool, then purée in a blender. Return mixture to saucepan. Purée sherry, avocados and cream in blender until smooth. Whisk into soup. Season to taste with black pepper and cayenne pepper.

Chill until ready to serve, then ladle into a chilled serving bowl and sprinkle with parsley.

Serves 6.

Tortilla Soup

2	tbsp.	vegetable oil	30	mL
1		medium onion, chopped	1	
1		garlic clove, minced	1	
14	oz.	can tomato sauce	398	mL
1/2	tsp.	ground cumin	2	mL
3³/4	cups	chicken broth OR 3 x 10 oz. (3 x 284 mL) cans	935	mL
2¹/2	cups	water OR 2 x 10 oz. (2 x 284 mL) cans	625	mL
1¹/2	cups	broken tortilla chips	375	mL
1	cup	shredded Monterey Jack cheese	250	mL
1		large tomato, chopped	1	

In a large stockpot, heat oil over medium heat and cook onion and garlic for 3 minutes. Add tomato sauce and cumin, heat to boiling, and simmer gently for 5 minutes. Add chicken broth and water, bring to a boil, and simmer for 5 minutes. Remove from heat.

To serve, divide tortilla chip pieces among soup bowls, pour soup over top and garnish with cheese and tomato.

Serves 6.

Pueblo Potato Soup

1	tbsp.	butter or margarine	15	mL
2		medium onions, chopped	2	
4		garlic cloves, minced	4	
2 x 4	oz.	cans chopped green chilies	2 x 114	mL
28	oz.	can chopped tomatoes	796	mL
6		medium potatoes, peeled, cut in 1/2" (1.3 cm) cubes	6	
2	cups	water	500	mL
2	cups	milk	500	mL
2	cups	shredded Cheddar cheese	500	mL

In a large stock pot, melt butter and sauté onions and garlic over medium heat. When onions are soft, add green chilies and tomatoes. Simmer 10 minutes, stirring frequently.

Add potatoes, water and milk. Cook for 20 minutes over medium heat, or until potatoes are done.

Add cheese and stir until melted. Simmer for 30 minutes on very low heat, stirring frequently.

Serves 6.

Salsa Corn Chowder

2	tbsp.	butter or margarine	30	mL
1		large onion, chopped	1	
1	tbsp.	flour	15	mL
1	tsp.	chili powder	5	mL
1	tsp.	ground cumin	5	mL
2	cups	frozen whole kernel corn, thawed	500	mL
2	cups	salsa	500	mL
1¼	cups	chicken broth OR 10 oz. (284 mL) can	300	mL
4	oz.	jar chopped pimiento, drained	114	mL
8	oz.	cream cheese, softened	250	mL
1	cup	milk	250	mL

Melt butter in a large saucepan, and sauté onions over medium heat until translucent.

Stir in flour and seasonings, then add corn, salsa, broth and pimiento. Bring to a boil; remove from heat.

Gradually add ¼ cup (60 mL) hot mixture to cream cheese in a small bowl, stirring until well blended. Add cream cheese mixture and milk to saucepan. Stir to combine and cook until thoroughly heated, being careful not to allow soup to boil. Serve immediately.

Serves 6.

Sopa De Verduras

Vegetable Soup

Stock:

7	cups	water	1.75	L
3	cups	chicken broth	750	mL
5		garlic cloves, minced	5	
1/2	tsp.	oregano	2	mL
2		whole cloves	2	
1	tbsp.	ground cumin	15	mL
1	tsp.	black pepper	5	mL
3		bay leaves	3	
1/2	tsp.	dried sweet basil	2	mL

Soup:

3	lb.	frying chicken, cut-up	1.5	kg
3		limes, juice of	3	
2		small zucchini, chopped	2	
1		onion, chopped	1	
3		jalapeño peppers, thinly sliced	3	
2		celery stalks, chopped	2	
1		carrot, chopped	1	
1		sweet green pepper, chopped	1	
14	oz.	can garbanzo beans, drained and rinsed	398	mL
1/2	cup	chopped cilantro	125	mL
4	cups	cooked rice (optional)	1	L

To make stock, bring water to a boil and add remaining stock ingredients and chicken. Simmer 1 1/2 hours, skimming foam from top. Remove chicken and allow to cool, then bone chicken and shred meat. Strain stock and chill.

To make soup, remove fat from stock. Reheat and add lime juice. Add all vegetables, except beans, and cook just until tender-crisp, about 30 minutes.

Add chicken and garbanzo beans. Heat until chicken and beans are thoroughly heated and serve immediately. Ladle into large soup bowls over 1/2 cup (125 mL) cooked rice per serving, if desired.

Serves 8.

Chorizo Bean Soup

1	lb.	chorizo sausage, see page 96	500	g
1		large onion, chopped	1	
3		carrots, chopped	3	
1	cup	chopped celery	250	mL
1	tbsp.	crushed red pepper	15	mL
14	oz.	can kidney beans, undrained	398	mL
2		large tomatoes, chopped	2	
3	cups	water	750	mL
1	tsp.	Worcestershire sauce	5	mL
1	tsp.	white vinegar	5	mL
		sour cream, for garnish		

In a large skillet, cook chorizo sausage over medium heat until browned; drain off excess liquid. Add onion, carrots and celery, and cook for 5 minutes.

Combine remaining ingredients, except sour cream, in a stock pot. Add chorizo mixture, bring to a boil and simmer for 30 minutes.

When serving, garnish each bowl with a dollop of sour cream.

Serves 6.

Sopa De Albóndigas

Meatball Soup

1	tbsp.	vegetable oil	15	mL
1		medium onion, thinly sliced	1	
4	cups	water	1	L
14	oz.	can chopped tomatoes, undrained	398	mL
1	tbsp.	chopped fresh parsley	15	mL
1	tsp.	dried oregano	5	mL
3 x 4	oz.	cans chopped green chilies	3 x 114	mL
6		green onions, chopped	6	
1	lb.	ground beef	500	g
1		egg	1	
1	tsp.	dried oregano	5	mL
1/4	cup	minced onion	60	mL

In a large saucepan, heat oil and sauté onion until translucent. Add water, tomatoes, parsley, oregano, green chilies and green onions. Bring to a boil and simmer, covered, for 10 minutes.

While soup is simmering, combine ground beef, egg, oregano and onion. Mix well. Form into 1" (2.5 cm) balls and drop into boiling broth. Boil, covered, over low heat for 30 minutes.

Serves 6.

Sopa De Mexicana

1/4	cup	butter or margarine	60	mL
2		garlic cloves, minced	2	
1		medium onion, chopped	1	
1		jalapeño pepper, finely chopped	1	
1/2	lb.	cooked ham, chopped	250	g
1		medium zucchini, chopped	1	
4 1/2	cups	beef broth	1.125	L
1/4	tsp	dried thyme	1	mL
2		large sweet red peppers, chopped	2	
5	oz.	can tomato paste	156	mL
14	oz.	can whole kernel corn, undrained	398	mL
		black pepper, to taste		
		chopped parsley, for garnish		

In a large stock pot, melt butter; add garlic, onion and jalapeño pepper and sauté over medium heat until onion is translucent. Add ham and zucchini and sauté for 10 minutes.

Add beef broth and thyme; simmer for 15 minutes. Add red peppers, tomato paste and corn; stir well and cook for 15 minutes more. Season with pepper and garnish with parsley to serve.

Serves 6.

Pollo Mexicana, page 77
Calabacitas Con Elote, page 106

Main Courses

Pepper Quesadillas

1½	tbsp.	vegetable oil	22	mL
1		large sweet green pepper, thinly sliced	1	
1		large sweet red pepper, thinly sliced	1	
1		large sweet yellow pepper, thinly sliced	1	
1		large onion, thinly sliced	1	
4	oz.	can chopped green chilies, drained	114	mL
½	tsp.	ground cumin	2	mL
6		8" (20 cm) flour tortillas	6	
2	cups	shredded Monterey Jack cheese	500	mL

Preheat oven to 425°F (220°C).

In a large skillet, over medium-high heat, heat oil and sauté peppers, onion and chilies for 5-7 minutes. Stir in cumin, then drain, reserving liquid.

Sprinkle half of each tortilla with cheese and top with pepper mixture. Fold tortillas in half and place on a baking sheet. Brush with reserved liquid. Bake 7-10 minutes, or until cheese is melted.

Cut each tortilla into thirds and serve warm with salsa, sour cream and/or guacamole.

Serves 6.

Pollo Mexicana

This recipe is intended to be a quick and easy, all-inclusive meal which is simplified further by the use of cheese spread.

2	tbsp.	butter or margarine	30	mL
1		garlic clove, minced	1	
2		whole boneless chicken breasts, skinned, halved	2	
4		green onions, chopped	4	
1		small sweet green pepper, chopped	1	
1		small sweet red pepper, chopped	1	
3	cups	cooked rice	750	mL
1/2	cup	cheese spread	125	mL
1	cup	salsa	250	mL

Melt butter in a large skillet over medium-high heat and sauté garlic for 2-3 minutes. Add chicken breasts and cook for 5 minutes. Turn chicken over and place green onions, green pepper and red pepper around edge of skillet; cook for 5 minutes, or until chicken is brown and thoroughly cooked.

Make a bed of rice on a serving platter and place chicken on top; cover and keep warm.

Add cheese spread and salsa to vegetables in skillet. Heat until cheese spread melts and sauce is hot. Pour over chicken and serve.

Serves 4.

Pictured on page 73

.

Chicken Gustoso

1/2	cup	chopped green onions	125	mL
2 x 4	oz.	cans chopped green chilies, drained	2 x 114	mL
1	cup	shredded Monterey Jack cheese	250	mL
2	tbsp.	butter or margarine, softened	30	mL
4		whole boneless chicken breasts skinned, halved	4	
1/4	cup	flour	60	mL
2		eggs, slightly beaten	2	
1	cup	seasoned bread crumbs	250	mL

Preheat oven to 350°F (180°C).

In a medium bowl, combine onions, chilies, cheese and butter. Place mixture on a sheet of wax paper and roll into a log. Chill.

Place chicken breasts between 2 pieces of wax paper and pound with the flat side of a wooden mallet until 1/8" (3 mm) thick. Peel off wax paper.

Cut chilled onion-cheese mixture into 8 equal pieces. Place a piece of the onion-cheese mixture at the end of one of the chicken cutlets. Roll in jelly-roll fashion, carefully tucking in the sides to encase the filling. Press to seal well and skewer with wooden toothpicks.

Dust with flour, dip in eggs and roll in bread crumbs. Repeat with remaining chicken cutlets.

Bake for 40-45 minutes.

Serves 8.

Pollo Con Queso

Chicken with Cheese Sauce

3	tbsp.	butter or margarine	45	mL
1		medium onion, chopped	1	
2		garlic cloves, minced	2	
1/4	cup	flour	60	mL
3	cups	cold milk	750	mL
3	cups	shredded Cheddar cheese	750	mL
2	tbsp.	chopped parsley	30	mL
5	oz.	can tomato paste	156	mL
1	tbsp.	chili powder	15	mL
1	tsp.	dried oregano	5	mL
4	oz.	can chopped green chilies, drained	114	mL
3		green onions, chopped	3	
		black pepper, to taste		
2	cups	cooked rice	500	mL
2	cups	diced, cooked chicken	500	mL
1	cup	coarsely crushed tortilla chips	250	mL

Preheat oven to 400°F (200°C).

In a large saucepan, melt butter over medium heat; cook onion and garlic until onion is translucent. Add flour and cook for 5 minutes, stirring constantly. Whisk in milk and cook for 10 minutes, or until sauce thickens, stirring constantly.

Remove from heat and add 2 cups (500 mL) of cheese; stir until melted. Stir in parsley, tomato paste, chili powder, oregano, green chilies, green onions and pepper.

Spread half of sauce in a 3-quart (3 L) casserole; top with rice, then chicken. Cover with remaining sauce. Bake, covered, for 40 minutes.

Sprinkle top with crushed tortilla chips and remaining cheese; bake for 10 additional minutes, or until cheese is bubbling.

Serves 6.

Chicken Casserole

2	cups	diced, cooked chicken	500	mL
1	cup	sour cream	250	mL
1	cup	salsa	250	mL
3		eggs	3	
1	tsp.	ground cumin	5	mL
1/2	tsp.	dried oregano	2	mL
4	oz.	can chopped green chilies, drained	114	mL
14	oz.	can refried beans	398	mL
6		10" (25 cm) flour tortillas	6	
1	cup	shredded Monterey Jack cheese	250	mL

Preheat oven to 350°F (180°C).

In a medium bowl, combine chicken, sour cream and salsa. Beat in eggs.

In a small bowl, stir cumin, oregano and chilies into refried beans.

Line a lightly greased 9 x 13" (23 x 33 cm) baking dish with 2 tortillas. Spoon half of the chicken mixture over tortillas and cover with 2 more tortillas. Spread all of the bean mixture on top and cover with remaining 2 tortillas. Spoon remaining chicken mixture over tortillas and top with cheese.

Bake for 45 minutes.

Serves 6.

Chicken Enchiladas

1		large onion, chopped	1	
1	tbsp.	vegetable oil	15	mL
4	cups	diced, cooked chicken	1	L
4	oz.	can chopped green chilies, drained	114	mL
10	oz.	can cream of chicken soup	284	mL
2	cups	shredded Cheddar cheese	500	mL
2	cups	shredded Monterey Jack cheese	500	mL
2	cups	salsa	500	mL
12-14		6" (15 cm) flour tortillas	12-14	

Preheat oven to 325°F (160°C).

In a large skillet, sauté onion in oil until translucent. Add chicken, chilies, soup and half of the cheeses. Cook over medium-low heat until cheese melts.

Divide chicken mixture evenly among tortillas, roll jelly-roll style, and place in a 9 x 13" (23 x 33 cm) baking dish, seam side down. Spread 1 cup (250 mL) salsa over bottom layer of enchiladas. Place remaining enchiladas on top, cover with 1 cup (250 mL) salsa and top with remaining cheeses.

Bake 30-40 minutes. Let stand 5 minutes before serving.

Serves 6.

Turkey Salad Burritos

2	cups	chopped, cooked turkey	500	mL
1		celery stalk, finely chopped	1	
1/2		large onion, finely chopped	1/2	
1/4	cup	sliced black olives	60	mL
1	cup	shredded Cheddar cheese	250	mL
1/2	cup	mayonnaise	125	mL
1/2	cup	salsa	125	mL
6		8" (20 cm) flour tortillas	6	

Preheat oven to 350°F (180°C).

In a medium bowl, combine turkey, celery, onion, black olives and cheese.

In another bowl, whisk together mayonnaise and salsa. Pour into turkey mixture and blend well. Spoon filling onto tortillas and fold burritos*.

Place burritos, seam side down, in a 9 x 13" (23 x 33 cm) baking dish and bake for 20 minutes, or until heated through, or microwave each burrito 2 1/2 minutes on high.

Serve with salsa and/or sour cream and garnish with black olives if desired.

Serves 6.

* See instructions to fold burritos on page 12.

Beef Enchiladas

1	lb.	ground beef	500	g
2		medium onions, chopped	2	
3		garlic cloves, minced	3	
1	tsp.	dried oregano	5	mL
1/2	tsp.	ground cumin	2	mL
1	tbsp.	chili powder	15	mL
1/4	tsp.	black pepper	1	mL
1	tsp.	crushed red pepper	5	mL
2 1/2	cups	shredded Monterey Jack cheese	625	mL
1	tbsp.	vegetable oil	15	mL
14	oz.	can tomato sauce	398	mL
1	cup	water	250	mL
2 1/2	tbsp.	chili powder	37	mL
1 1/2	tsp.	ground cumin	7	mL
12		8" (20 cm) flour tortillas	12	

Preheat oven to 350°F (180°C).

In a large skillet, brown ground beef, onions and 1 garlic clove; drain off excess liquid. Add oregano, 1/2 tsp. (2 mL) cumin, 1 tbsp. (15 mL) chili powder, black pepper and crushed red pepper. Add 2 cups (500 mL) cheese, remove from heat and allow cheese to melt through the filling mixture.

Sauté remaining 2 garlic cloves in oil in a saucepan. Add tomato sauce, water, 2 1/2 tbsp. (37 mL) chili powder and 1 1/2 tsp. (7 mL) cumin. Bring to a boil, cover and simmer 10 minutes.

Spread each tortilla with 1-2 tbsp. (15-30 mL) of sauce. Spread 1 heaping tbsp. (30 mL) of filling on each tortilla. Roll jelly-roll style and lay in a single layer, seam side down, in a lightly greased 9 x 13" (23 x 33 cm) baking dish. Cover with remaining sauce. Sprinkle remaining cheese on top and bake for 30-40 minutes.

Makes 12 enchiladas, to serve 6.

Burritos

1	lb.	ground beef	500	g
1		medium onion, chopped	1	
1		garlic clove, minced	1	
14	oz.	can refried beans	398	mL
1	tsp.	dried oregano	5	mL
3/4	tsp.	ground cumin	3	mL
1	tbsp.	chili powder	15	mL
1/4	tsp.	black pepper	1	mL
1	tsp.	crushed red pepper	5	mL
1	tbsp.	chopped parsley	15	mL
1/4	cup	sour cream	60	mL
2	cups	shredded Monterey Jack cheese	500	mL
1 1/2	cups	salsa	375	mL
10		10" (25 cm) flour tortillas	10	

Preheat oven to 350°F (180°C).

In a large skillet, brown ground beef, onions and garlic; drain off excess liquid. Add beans, spices, parsley, sour cream, 1 cup (250 mL) of cheese and 1 cup (250 mL) of salsa. Stir to combine and heat until cheese is melted.

Divide beef mixture evenly among tortillas, approximately 1/2 cup (125 mL) each, and fold burritos.* Place in a 9 x 13" (23 x 33 cm) baking dish, seam side down. Sprinkle with remaining cheese and top with remaining salsa. Bake for 20 minutes.

Serves 6.

* See instructions to fold burritos on page 12.

Tamale Pie

1	lb.	ground beef	500	g
1		large onion, chopped	1	
2		garlic cloves, minced	2	
28	oz.	can tomatoes	796	mL
14	oz.	can kernel corn, drained	398	mL
2	tbsp.	chili powder	30	mL
1/2	tsp.	dried oregano	2	mL
1/2	tsp.	ground cumin	2	mL

Cornmeal Topping:

3/4	cup	cornmeal	175	mL
1	cup	flour	250	mL
1/3	cup	sugar	75	mL
1	tbsp.	baking powder	15	mL
1	cup	milk	250	mL
1		egg, well beaten	1	
2	tbsp.	melted butter or margarine	30	mL
1 1/2	cups	shredded Cheddar cheese	375	mL

Preheat oven to 350°F (180°C).

In a large skillet, brown ground beef, onion and garlic over medium-high heat; drain off excess liquid. Stir in tomatoes, corn, and spices. Cover and simmer 10 minutes.

Spread mixture in a shallow 3-quart (3 L) casserole. Set aside and prepare the cornmeal topping.

In a small bowl, combine cornmeal, flour, sugar and baking powder. In another bowl, combine milk, egg and butter. Stir the egg mixture into the flour mixture.

Spoon topping over meat mixture and sprinkle with cheese. Bake, uncovered, for 45 minutes, or until top is set when lightly touched.

Serves 6.

Hot Mexican Meatballs

Meatballs:

2		eggs	2	
2	lbs.	ground beef	1	kg
1		large onion, finely chopped	1	
2		garlic cloves, minced	2	
1/3	cup	ground almonds	75	mL
1	cup	breadcrumbs	250	mL
1	tbsp.	dried parsley	15	mL
1	tsp.	cinnamon	5	mL
1/2	tsp.	black pepper	2	mL

Jalapeño Tomato Sauce:

1	tbsp.	vegetable oil	15	mL
1		large onion, finely chopped	1	
1		garlic clove, minced	1	
1/2	tbsp.	brown sugar	7	mL
14	oz.	can stewed tomatoes	398	mL
1		sweet green pepper, thinly sliced	1	
1		sweet red pepper, thinly sliced	1	
3		jalapeño peppers, finely chopped	3	
1/2	tsp.	cayenne pepper	2	mL
1	tsp.	paprika	5	mL
1	tbsp.	dried parsley	15	mL
1/2	cup	beef stock	125	mL
		black pepper, to taste		
2	tsp.	cornstarch	10	mL
1/4	cup	water	60	mL

In a large mixing bowl, lightly beat eggs. Add remaining ingredients and mix well.

Shape meat mixture into walnut-sized balls and brown in a nonstick frying pan, turning occasionally. Set aside while preparing Jalapeño Tomato Sauce.

Hot Mexican Meatballs

Continued

To prepare sauce, heat oil over medium-high heat in a large saucepan. Cook onion, garlic and brown sugar, stirring occasionally, until onion is soft. Add tomatoes, green, red and jalapeño peppers, cayenne pepper, paprika and parsley; cook for 3 minutes, stirring occasionally. Pour in beef stock and season with pepper. Increase heat to high and bring sauce to a boil. Boil for 1 minute, then reduce heat to low. Combine cornstarch and water; stir to make a smooth paste and add to sauce.

Add meatballs to sauce, cover pan, and continue cooking for 20-25 minutes. Transfer meatballs and sauce to a warmed serving dish and serve immediately.

Serves 8.

Grilled Fajitas

12	oz.	bottle beer	341	mL
1/4	cup	soy sauce	60	mL
4		garlic cloves, minced	4	
1	tsp.	ground cumin	5	mL
1	tsp.	chili powder	5	mL
1	tsp.	Tabasco sauce	5	mL
4		tenderloin steaks *	4	
1/4	tsp.	black pepper	1	mL
2	tbsp.	vegetable oil	30	mL
2		large onions, thinly sliced	2	
1		large sweet green pepper, cut in 1/2" (1.3 cm) strips	1	
1		large sweet red pepper, cut in 1/2" (1.3 cm) strips	1	
1		large sweet yellow pepper, cut in 1/2" (1.3 cm) strips	1	
2		limes, cut in wedges	2	
8		6" (15 cm) flour tortillas	8	
		salsa		
		sour cream		

Combine beer, soy sauce, garlic, cumin, chili powder and Tabasco sauce in a large nonmetallic dish. Add beef; cover dish and marinate in refrigerator for at least 2 hours, turning beef several times. Remove beef from marinade and season with black pepper.

Oil barbecue grill before igniting to help prevent sticking. Grill beef over medium heat until steak reaches desired doneness, turning once.

While steak is cooking, heat oil and stir-fry vegetables over medium-high heat, either on barbecue or on stove top, until tender. Slice beef into 1/2" (1.3 cm) strips, cut against the grain, and squeeze juice from lime wedges over beef strips. Serve in heated tortillas with vegetables, salsa and sour cream (fold filled tortillas burrito-style as on page 12).

Serves 4.

* For a more tender cut of steak, buy a whole beef tenderloin and slice your own steaks. It works out to be much cheaper than buying sirloin or T-bone steaks, and the meat is more tender.

Grilled Fajitas

Continued

Note: To add extra flavor to your barbecued foods, try soaking mesquite or hickory wood chips, fresh rosemary sprigs, orange peel, garlic cloves, fennel pieces, or onions, etc. in water for 20 minutes, then placing them directly on barbecue coals or bricks. They'll smoke and smolder, not burn.

Chili Con Carne

1½	lbs.	ground beef	750	g
1		large onion, chopped	1	
3		garlic cloves, minced	3	
4		celery stalks, chopped	4	
1		large sweet green pepper, chopped	1	
1		large sweet red pepper, chopped	1	
3		Anaheim peppers, chopped	3	
3		jalapeño peppers, sliced	3	
28	oz.	can stewed tomatoes	796	mL
14	oz.	can tomato paste	398	mL
2 x14	oz.	cans dark kidney beans, undrained	2 x 398	mL
½	lb.	fresh mushrooms, sliced	250	g
2	tbsp.	brown sugar	30	mL
2	tbsp.	white vinegar	30	mL
1	cup	salsa	250	mL
¼	cup	chili powder	60	mL
1	tsp.	crushed red pepper	5	mL
½	tsp.	each cayenne pepper & black pepper	2	mL
½	tsp.	ground cumin	2	mL
3		whole dried chilies	3	
1	tsp.	Tabasco sauce	5	mL
		shredded Cheddar cheese, for garnish		

In a large skillet over medium heat, brown ground beef, onion and garlic; drain off excess liquid. Add celery and peppers, and cook for 10 minutes. Meanwhile, combine all other ingredients in a large stock pot. Add beef mixture; cook over medium heat until chili comes to a boil. Reduce heat to low; simmer for 20-30 minutes. Remove whole dried chilies. Serve topped with Cheddar cheese.

Mexican Lasagne

1¹/₂	lbs.	ground beef	750	g
1		large onion, chopped	1	
2		garlic cloves, minced	2	
1¹/₂	tsp.	ground cumin	7	mL
2	tbsp.	chili powder	30	mL
¹/₂	tsp.	cayenne pepper	2	mL
¹/₄	tsp.	crushed red pepper	1	mL
14	oz.	can stewed tomatoes	398	mL
12		6" (15 cm) corn tortillas	12	
2	cups	ricotta cheese	500	mL
1	cup	shredded Monterey Jack cheese	250	mL
1		egg, slightly beaten	1	
¹/₂	cup	shredded Cheddar cheese	125	mL
1	cup	shredded lettuce	250	mL
1		large tomato, chopped	1	
4		green onions, chopped	4	
¹/₂	cup	chopped olives	125	mL

Preheat oven to 350°F (180°C).

In a large skillet, brown ground beef, onion and garlic. Add spices and tomatoes; heat thoroughly.

Cover bottom and sides of a lightly greased 9 x 13" (23 x 33 cm) baking dish with half the tortillas. Spread beef mixture over tortillas and top with remaining tortillas; set aside.

Combine ricotta cheese, Monterey Jack cheese and egg; spread over tortillas. Bake for 30-40 minutes.

Remove from oven and sprinkle top with diagonal rows of shredded Cheddar cheese, lettuce, tomatoes, green onions and olives.

Serves 8.

Pictured on page 91.

Mexican Lasagne, page 90

Pasta Tacos

1½	lbs.	ground beef	750	g
4	oz.	cream cheese, softened	125	g
1	tbsp.	chili powder	15	mL
1	tsp.	ground cumin	5	mL
18		jumbo pasta shells, cooked, drained	18	
1	cup	salsa	250	mL
1	cup	shredded Cheddar cheese	250	mL
1	cup	shredded Monterey Jack cheese	250	mL
1½	cups	finely crushed tortilla chips	375	mL
1	cup	sour cream	250	mL
3		green onions, chopped	3	

Preheat oven to 350°F (180°C).

Cook beef in a large skillet over medium-high heat until brown; drain off excess liquid. Reduce heat to medium-low and add cream cheese, chili powder and cumin; simmer 5 minutes.

Fill shells with beef mixture and arrange in a lightly greased 9 x 13" (23 x 33 cm) baking dish. Pour salsa over each shell. Cover dish with foil and bake for 15 minutes.

Remove foil and sprinkle each shell with cheeses and crushed chips. Bake 15 minutes more, or until cheese is bubbly.

To serve, top each shell with a dollop of sour cream and sprinkle with green onions.

Serves 4.

Jalapeño Pork Chops

2		jalapeño peppers, finely chopped	2	
1		medium onion, chopped	1	
2		garlic cloves, minced	2	
1	tbsp.	vegetable oil	15	mL
1/2	cup	shredded Monterey Jack cheese	125	mL
6		pork chops, cut 1-2" (2.5-5 cm) thick	6	

In a medium skillet over medium heat, sauté jalapeño peppers, onion and garlic in vegetable oil until soft. Remove from heat and cool. Stir in cheese.

Slice into one side of each pork chop horizontally, creating a pocket. Be careful not to cut through the other 3 sides. Stuff pork chops with jalapeno mixture and close opening with a toothpick.

Grill pork chops on barbecue to desired doneness.

Serves 6.

Presidente Pork Roast

5	lb.	boneless pork roast	2.2	kg
1/2	tsp.	garlic powder	2	mL
1/2	tsp.	chili powder	2	mL
1/2	cup	apple jelly	125	mL
1/2	cup	ketchup	125	mL
1	tbsp.	vinegar	15	mL
1/2	tsp.	chili powder	2	mL
1/2	cup	finely crushed tortilla chips	125	mL

Preheat oven to 325°F (160°C)

Place pork, fat side up, in a shallow roasting pan. Combine garlic powder and 1/2 tsp. (2 mL) chili powder and rub into roast. Bake for 2-2 1/2 hours.

In a small saucepan, combine jelly, ketchup, vinegar and remaining 1/2 tsp. (2 mL) chili powder. Bring to a boil, then reduce heat and simmer, uncovered, for 2 minutes.

Brush roast with glaze and sprinkle top with tortilla chips. Continue roasting for 10-15 minutes. Remove roast from oven and let stand 10 minutes before carving.

Serve glaze as a sauce with roast.

Serves 8.

Chorizo

Chorizo is a very popular addition to many Mexican and Spanish dishes. This highly spiced pork sausage is used in soups, stews, enchiladas and casseroles. It is not always available in North American supermarkets, so now you can make your own.

1	lb.	ground pork	500	g
1		large onion, chopped	1	
2		garlic cloves, minced	2	
1		jalapeño pepper, chopped	1	
1	tsp.	dried oregano	5	mL
1/2	tsp.	ground cumin	2	mL
1	tbsp.	chili powder	15	mL
1/4	tsp.	black pepper	1	mL
1	tsp.	crushed red pepper	5	mL

Place ground pork in a large bowl.

Place onion, garlic and jalapeños in a blender and chop until very fine. Add spices to blender and purée.

Add onion mixture to pork and mix well. At this point, chorizo can be frozen for future use or cooked to use in other recipes.

Makes 1 lb. (500 g) of sausage meat.

Note: In the recipes in this book, chorizo sausage is used as a ground meat rather than being shaped into sausage casings.

Vegetables & Side Dishes

Pepper Pasta Salad

1½	cups	uncooked rotini pasta	375	mL
1		large onion, thinly sliced	1	
1		large sweet green pepper, thinly sliced	1	
1		large sweet red pepper, thinly sliced	1	
1		large sweet yellow pepper, thinly sliced	1	
4		garlic cloves, minced	4	
2	tbsp.	vegetable oil	30	mL
1	tsp.	dried sweet basil	5	mL
½	tsp.	dried oregano	2	mL
⅔	cup	salsa	150	mL
2	tbsp.	balsamic vinegar	30	mL
¼	cup	grated Parmesan cheese	60	mL

Cook pasta according to package directions and drain.

In a large skillet, heat oil and cook onion, peppers and garlic over medium-high heat, stirring frequently, for about 5 minutes. Add herbs and continue cooking until vegetables are tender. Add salsa and vinegar and cook for 2 minutes, stirring occasionally.

In a serving dish, add pepper mixture to pasta; sprinkle with cheese, toss and serve. This salad is also delicious when served cold.

Serves 6.

Pasta Picante

2	tbsp.	vegetable oil	30	mL
1		medium onion, thinly sliced	1	
3		garlic cloves, minced	3	
2		large tomatoes, chopped	2	
1		large sweet green pepper, chopped	1	
3/4	cup	salsa	175	mL
14	oz.	can pitted black olives, drained, sliced	398	mL
1	tsp.	ground cumin	5	mL
1	tsp.	chili powder	5	mL
1½	cups	uncooked rotini or penne pasta	375	mL
1	cup	shredded Monterey Jack cheese	250	mL

In a large skillet, heat oil and cook onion and garlic over medium heat until onion is translucent. Add tomatoes, green pepper, salsa, olives, cumin and chili powder. Bring to a boil; reduce heat and simmer, stirring frequently, for 10-12 minutes, or until peppers are tender and sauce has thickened.

While sauce simmers, cook pasta according to package directions and drain.

In serving dish, pour sauce over pasta, toss and sprinkle with cheese before serving. This dish may be served hot or cold.

Serves 6.

Arroz Verde

2	cups	long-grain rice, uncooked	500	mL
3	tbsp.	vegetable oil	45	mL
1		small onion, chopped	1	
1/2		large sweet red pepper, chopped	1/2	
1/2		large sweet yellow pepper, chopped	1/2	
4		jalapeño peppers, chopped	4	
2		garlic cloves, minced	2	
4	cups	chicken broth	1	L

Preheat oven to 350°F (180°C).

In a large saucepan or skillet, heat oil and sauté rice over medium heat for 2 minutes. Add onion and red and yellow pepper; continue cooking until peppers are soft and rice is golden brown, about 5-7 minutes.

In a blender, purée jalapeños, garlic and 1/2 cup (125 mL) of chicken broth until smooth. Add to rice and cook over low heat for 5 minutes. Stir in remaining broth and transfer to a 2-quart (2 L) casserole. Cover and bake for 45 minutes. Fluff rice with a fork prior to serving.

Serves 6.

Cumin Rice

2	tbsp.	vegetable oil	30	mL
1		medium sweet green pepper, finely chopped	1	
1		medium sweet red pepper, finely chopped	1	
4		green onions, chopped	4	
1		garlic clove, minced	1	
1	cup	long-grain rice, uncooked	250	mL
3/4	tsp.	ground cumin	3	mL
2	cups	chicken broth	500	mL

Preheat oven to 350°F (180°C).

Heat oil in a medium skillet. Add peppers, onion, garlic and rice. Cook until rice is lightly browned and onion is translucent, about 5 minutes. Transfer rice mixture to a 2-quart (2 L) casserole, and add cumin and chicken broth. Cover tightly and bake for 30 minutes, or until all liquid is absorbed.

Serves 4.

Mexican Rice

1	tbsp.	vegetable oil	15	mL
1		large onion, chopped	1	
1	cup	long-grain rice, uncooked	250	mL
28	oz.	can stewed tomatoes	796	mL
1/2		medium sweet green pepper, chopped	1/2	
1/2		medium sweet red pepper, chopped	1/2	
2	tsp.	chili powder	10	mL
1/4	tsp.	cayenne pepper	1	mL
1/2	cup	water	125	mL

In a large skillet, heat oil and add onion and rice. Sauté for 5 minutes, or until onion is translucent and rice is evenly browned, stirring frequently. Add remaining ingredients and mix well. Cover and simmer until rice is tender, approximately 30 minutes. Remove lid and continue cooking until liquid is absorbed.

Serves 6.

Chili Relleno Bake

Stuffed Baked Chilies

1	tbsp.	vegetable oil	15	mL
1		large onion, chopped	1	
2		garlic cloves, minced	2	
14	oz.	can tomato sauce	398	mL
1/2	tsp.	dried oregano	2	mL
		Tabasco sauce, to taste		
4 x 4	oz.	cans whole green chilies, drained	4 x 114	mL
2	cups	shredded Monterey Jack cheese	500	mL

Preheat oven to 350°F (180°C).

In a large skillet, heat oil and cook onion and garlic until onion is translucent. Add tomato sauce, oregano and Tabasco sauce. Simmer until heated through.

Line a 9" (23 cm) square baking dish with half of the chilies, splitting each chili up one side and opening to lay flat; top with 1 1/2 cups (375 mL) of shredded Monterey Jack cheese. Top with remaining split chilies, then pour tomato sauce over all.

Bake, uncovered, for 30 minutes.

Sprinkle remaining 1/2 cup (125 mL) cheese on top. Let stand 5 minutes before serving.

Serves 6.

Chilies Con Nogadas

Chilies with Almonds

1	cup	shredded Cheddar cheese	250	mL
1	cup	shredded Swiss cheese	250	mL
1	cup	ricotta cheese	250	mL
1½	cups	chopped, cooked ham	375	mL
1		small jalapeño pepper, finely chopped	1	
½	cup	slivered almonds	125	mL
1	tbsp.	brown sugar	15	mL
½	tsp.	cinnamon	2	mL
⅛	tsp.	ground cloves	0.5	mL
⅛	tsp.	ground cumin	0.5	mL
4 x 4	oz.	cans whole green chilies, drained	4 x 114	mL

Preheat oven to 350°F (180°C).

In a large bowl, mix together all ingredients except canned chilies. Separate chilies on a flat work surface. Run a finger inside each chili to open, being careful not to tear. Gently pack each chile with stuffing.

Place stuffed chilies in a lightly greased 9" (23 cm) square baking dish in a single layer. Bake for 20 minutes, or until cheeses have melted.

Serves 6.

Okra and Chilies

2	tbsp.	butter or margarine	30	mL
1½	tsp.	chili powder	7	mL
½	tsp.	ground cumin	2	mL
½	tsp.	Italian seasoning	2	mL
4		garlic cloves, minced	4	
2		medium onions, sliced into rings	2	
2		tomatoes, chopped	2	
6		jalapeño peppers, cut into thin rings	6	
1		large sweet red pepper, cut into thin strips	1	
2 x 14	oz.	cans okra, drained	2 x 398	mL
		pepper, to taste		
1	cup	shredded Cheddar cheese	250	mL
2		strips cooked bacon, crumbled	2	
1		jalapeño pepper, cut into thin rings	1	

Preheat oven to 350°F (180°C).

In a large skillet over medium-high heat, melt butter or margarine. Add chili powder, cumin, Italian seasoning and garlic; stir rapidly for about 1 minute. Add onions, tomatoes, 6 jalapeños, red pepper and okra, and stir to mix well. Reduce heat to simmer; cover and cook until onions and peppers are tender. Season to taste with pepper.

Transfer pepper mixture to a 9 x 13" (23 x 33 cm) baking dish. Sprinkle with cheese, crumbled bacon and remaining jalapeño pepper. Bake for 15 minutes and serve immediately.

Serves 4.

Pepper Pot

1	tbsp.	vegetable oil	15	mL
1		large onion, chopped	1	
1		medium sweet green pepper, thinly sliced	1	
1		medium sweet yellow pepper, thinly sliced	1	
1		medium sweet orange pepper, thinly sliced	1	
1		medium sweet red pepper, thinly sliced	1	
4		garlic cloves, minced	4	
1 1/2	tsp.	ground cumin	7	mL
1	tsp.	ground coriander	5	mL
1	tsp.	dry mustard	5	mL
1/2	tsp.	cayenne pepper	2	mL
1/2	tsp.	black pepper	2	mL
2	tbsp.	flour	30	mL
3		large eggs	3	
2	cups	sour cream	500	mL
2	cups	shredded Cheddar cheese	500	mL
		cayenne pepper, for color		

Preheat oven to 375°F (190°C) and lightly grease a 10" (25 cm) square baking dish or equivalent-sized casserole.

Heat vegetable oil in a large skillet. Add onions and sauté over medium heat until onions are translucent. Add green, yellow, orange and red peppers, garlic, cumin, coriander, mustard, cayenne pepper and black pepper. Sauté an additional 10 minutes, then sprinkle with flour. Cook and stir for 5 minutes, or until the peppers are very tender. Place cooked pepper mixture in the prepared baking dish.

Beat together eggs and sour cream. Pour egg mixture over the peppers. Top with Cheddar cheese and sprinkle with cayenne pepper, for color.

Bake, uncovered, for 45 minutes, or until firm in the center and bubbling around the edges.

Serves 6.

Calabacitas Con Elote

2	tbsp.	butter or margarine	30	mL
1		medium onion, chopped	1	
2		garlic cloves, minced	2	
4		medium zucchini, scrubbed, cubed	4	
10	oz.	can whole kernel corn, drained	298	mL
1		medium sweet red pepper, chopped	1	
1		jalapeño pepper, finely chopped	1	
		black pepper, to taste		

In a large skillet, melt butter over medium heat and sauté onion and garlic until onion is translucent. Add zucchini, corn, red and jalapeño peppers. Cook, stirring often, for 5 minutes, or until vegetables are tender-crisp. Add black pepper and serve immediately.

Serves 8.

Pictured on page 73.

Hominy Heat

4		slices bacon, chopped	4	
1		small onion, chopped	1	
4	oz.	can chopped green chilies, drained	114	mL
2 x 14	oz.	cans yellow or white hominy*, drained	2 x 398	mL
1	tbsp.	chili powder	15	mL
14	oz.	can tomato sauce	398	mL

In a large skillet over medium heat, cook chopped bacon until done but not crisp; drain off fat. Add onion and green chilies and cook for 5 minutes. Add hominy, chili powder and tomato sauce and stir until well combined. Cover and simmer over low heat for 20 minutes, stirring occasionally. Serve immediately.

Serves 6.

* Hominy is a native American Indian food made from dried white or yellow corn kernels.

Mexicali Corn

1	tbsp.	vegetable oil	15	mL
1/2		large sweet green pepper, chopped	1/2	
1/2		large sweet red pepper, chopped	1/2	
1		jalapeño pepper, finely chopped	1	
14	oz.	can whole kernel corn, drained	398	mL
1		large tomato, chopped	1	
1/4	tsp.	black pepper	1	mL

Heat oil in a medium saucepan. Sauté green, red and jalapeño peppers over medium heat for 5 minutes. Add corn, tomato and black pepper and heat thoroughly. Serve immediately.

Serves 4.

Grilled Vegetable Kabobs

1/4	cup	olive oil	60	mL
2	tbsp.	red wine vinegar	30	mL
1	tsp.	crushed red pepper	5	mL
1	tsp.	dried parsley	5	mL
1/2	tsp.	ground cumin	2	mL
4		ears corn on the cob, cut into 2" (5 cm) lengths	4	
1		large sweet green pepper, cut into wedges	1	
1		large sweet red pepper, cut into wedges	1	
2		large onions, cut into wedges	2	
2		medium zucchini, cut into 1" (2.5 cm) rounds	2	
12		cherry tomatoes	12	

In a small saucepan, combine oil, vinegar, crushed pepper, parsley, and cumin. Bring to a boil and simmer for 10-15 minutes.

Thread the vegetables on skewers and brush with the pepper sauce. Grill on a preheated barbecue over medium heat for 10-20 minutes, or until done, basting frequently.

Serves 6.

Note: If using wooden skewers, soak them in water before threading on the vegetables.

Clockwise from the top right

Papaya Salsa, page 121
Mango Salsa, page 120
Salsa Fresca, page 120
Salsa Especial, page 119

Cheddar Chili Tomatoes

6		medium tomatoes	6	
3¹/₂	cups	shredded Cheddar cheese	875	mL
2 x 4	oz.	cans chopped green chilies, drained	2 x 114	mL
¹/₂	tsp.	dried oregano	2	mL
2		garlic cloves, minced	2	
6	tbsp.	sour cream	90	mL
3		green onions, chopped	3	

Preheat oven to 325°F (160°C).

Lightly grease a shallow 9" (23 cm) square baking dish. Cut a ¹/₂" (1.3 cm) slice from the top of each tomato and scoop out pulp and seeds, leaving a ¹/₄" (6 mm) shell. Invert tomatoes on a paper towel and let drain for 20 minutes.

Combine cheese, chilies, oregano and garlic in a medium bowl. Divide mixture evenly among tomato shells. Arrange tomato shells in prepared dish and bake for 20 minutes.

To serve, top each tomato with a dollop of sour cream and sprinkle with green onions.

Serves 6.

Refried Beans

14	oz.	can red kidney beans, drained	398	mL
1/2	cup	salsa	125	mL
1/2	cup	shredded Cheddar cheese	125	mL
1		garlic clove, minced	1	
2	tbsp.	minced onion	30	mL

Mash beans in a small saucepan. Add remaining ingredients and heat until cheese is melted.

Makes about 2 cups (500 mL) to serve 4.

Green Beans Mexicana

2 1/2	cups	fresh or frozen green beans	625	mL
2	tbsp.	butter or margarine	30	mL
1	tsp.	dried sweet basil	5	mL
1/4	tsp.	black pepper	1	mL
2	tbsp.	lime juice	30	mL
1/4	cup	sliced almonds, toasted *	60	mL

Cook beans until tender-crisp; drain well.

Melt butter in a large skillet over medium heat. Add beans, basil, and pepper and cook, stirring constantly, for 5 minutes. Add lime juice and toasted almonds. Mix well and serve immediately.

Serves 4.

* To toast almonds, place in a nonstick frying pan and cook, stirring often, on stove top over medium heat until lightly browned.

Cauliflower Mexicana

1		medium cauliflower	1	
1	tbsp.	butter or margarine	15	mL
1		medium onion, chopped	1	
5	oz.	can tomato paste	156	mL
5	oz.	can of water	156	mL
1	tsp.	chili powder	5	mL
2	tbsp.	chopped fresh parsley	30	mL
3	tbsp.	breadcrumbs	45	mL
3	tbsp.	grated Parmesan cheese	45	mL

Preheat oven to 350°F (180°C).

Break cauliflower into florets and cook until tender-crisp. Drain well.

While the cauliflower is cooking, melt butter in a medium skillet over low heat; add onion and cook until translucent. Add tomato paste, water, chili powder and parsley. Stir and bring mixture to a boil over medium heat.

Transfer to a 2-quart (2 L) casserole, add cauliflower and stir. Sprinkle top with breadcrumbs and cheese and bake, uncovered, for 10-15 minutes, or until top is golden brown.

Serves 6.

Golden Mexi-Fries

6		large baking potatoes, scrubbed	6	
1/4	cup	flour	60	mL
1/4	cup	Parmesan cheese	60	mL
1/2	tsp.	cayenne pepper	2	mL
1	tbsp.	dried parsley	15	mL
		seasoned salt, to taste		
		seasoned pepper, to taste		

Preheat oven to 350°F (180°C).

Cut potatoes lengthwise into 8 wedges.

Combine all dry ingredients in a plastic bag; add potatoes and shake to coat completely.

Place potatoes on a lightly greased cookie sheet and bake for 1 hour, or until golden brown, turning occasionally.

Serves 6.

Mexi-Stuffed Potatoes

6		large potatoes	6	
1/2	cup	softened butter or margarine	125	mL
1	cup	shredded Cheddar cheese	250	mL
1	cup	hot milk	250	mL
1	tbsp.	minced onion	15	mL
1		garlic clove, minced	1	
1	tsp.	chili powder	5	mL
1/2		large sweet green pepper, finely chopped	1/2	
2		jalapeño peppers, finely chopped	2	

Preheat oven to 350°F (180°C).

Scrub and bake potatoes until tender, about 50-60 minutes.

Allow potatoes to cool until they are easy to handle. Cut potatoes in half lengthwise and scoop out pulp into a bowl, being careful not to break skins. Add butter, cheese, milk, onion, garlic and spices, and beat with electric mixer until smooth. Stir in chopped peppers.

Stuff potato shells with filling and arrange on a baking sheet. Bake for 15-20 minutes.

Serves 8.

Spicy Topped Potatoes

4		large baking potatoes	4	
1/4	cup	butter or margarine	60	mL
4		jalapeño peppers, finely chopped	4	
1/4	cup	flour	60	mL
1/2	tsp.	dry mustard	2	mL
1/4	tsp.	cayenne pepper	1	mL
1/4	tsp.	paprika	1	mL
1/4	tsp.	black pepper	1	mL
1 1/2	cups	milk	375	mL
1	cup	shredded Cheddar cheese	250	mL
1	cup	broccoli florets	250	mL

Preheat oven to 350°F (180°C).

Scrub and bake potatoes until tender, about 50-60 minutes.

While potatoes are baking, melt butter in a medium saucepan over medium-low heat. Add jalapeño peppers and cook for 1 minute. Add flour and seasonings and stir until well blended. Gradually add milk, stirring constantly, until mixture is thickened. Remove from heat and add cheese, stirring until melted. Cover and keep warm.

Cook broccoli florets for 1 minute, or until tender-crisp, and drain off excess water.

Slice cooked potatoes lengthwise, score insides, and place potato halves on serving dish. Evenly distribute broccoli on top of potatoes and drizzle with cheese sauce. Serve immediately.

Serves 6.

Preserves, Salsas & Sauces

Jalapeño Pepper Jelly

3		sweet green peppers, finely chopped	3	
1	cup	finely chopped jalapeño peppers	250	mL
1½	cups	white vinegar	375	mL
6½	cups	sugar	1.625	L
1	tsp.	cayenne pepper	5	mL
6	oz.	bottle Certo liquid	170	mL
6		drops green food coloring	6	

In a large pot, combine green and jalapeño peppers with vinegar, sugar and cayenne pepper. Cook over medium-high heat, stirring frequently, until mixture begins to boil.

Add Certo and boil 5 minutes longer, stirring constantly. Remove from heat, skim off foam and pour into sterilized jars.

To serve, spoon jelly over a block of cream cheese and serve with tortilla chips, crackers and/or raw vegetables.

Makes 8-9, 6 oz. (170 mL) jars.

Salsa Especial

7	lbs.	Roma or plum tomatoes	3	kg
4		celery stalks, finely chopped	4	
2		large sweet green peppers, finely chopped	2	
2		large sweet red peppers, finely chopped	2	
8		jalapeño peppers, finely chopped	8	
3		large onions, finely chopped	3	
1/4	cup	chopped cilantro or parsley	60	mL
5		garlic cloves, minced	5	
4 x 4	oz.	cans chopped green chilies, drained	4 x 114	mL
14	oz.	can tomato paste	398	mL
6		drops Tabasco sauce	6	
3/4	cup	white vinegar	175	mL
2	tbsp.	sugar	30	mL
2	tbsp.	paprika	30	mL
1	tbsp.	cayenne pepper	15	mL

Coarsely chop tomatoes and place in a very large stock pot. Add all other ingredients to tomatoes and simmer vegetables until tender-crisp, about 1/2 hour.

Ladle salsa into sterilized canning jars, filling to 1/2" (1.3 cm) from top. Cover immediately with sterilized lids and screw bands. Place in boiling water bath and process for 20 minutes for pint jars and 25 minutes for quart jars. Remove jars from water and cool.

Makes 8 pint, 2 cup (500 mL) jars of salsa.

Note: Feel free to experiment with some of the different varieties of peppers and chilies that are seasonally available. If you like salsa with a bite, don't be afraid to add more hot stuff! This recipe is very flexible and doubles, triples, etc. extremely well. The largest batch to date was 14 times the original recipe! Take liberty with the quantities of vegetables and spices used.

Pictured on page 109.

Salsa Fresca

6		jalapeño peppers, finely chopped	6	
1		small onion, chopped	1	
4		medium tomatoes, chopped	4	
2		garlic cloves, minced	2	
1/4	cup	finely chopped cilantro	60	mL
2	tbsp.	lime juice	30	mL

In a nonmetallic bowl, stir together all ingredients. Refrigerate overnight. Serve with tortilla chips as a snack or as a condiment with barbecued meat.

Makes about 3 cups (750 mL) of salsa.

Pictured on page 109.

Mango Salsa

1		large ripe mango*, peeled, diced	1	
1		slice onion, finely chopped	1	
1/2		large sweet red pepper, finely chopped	1/2	
1	tbsp.	finely chopped fresh mint	15	mL

In a small bowl, combine all ingredients and refrigerate overnight. Excellent with grilled chicken or fish.

Makes about 2 cups (500 mL) of salsa.

* If fresh mango isn't available, substitute a 14 oz. (398 mL) can of mangoes, drained and diced.

Pictured on page 109.

Papaya Salsa

1		large ripe papaya*, peeled, chopped	1	
1		small sweet red pepper, chopped	1	
1		small red onion, chopped	1	
1/4	cup	chopped cilantro	60	mL
1		jalapeño pepper, finely chopped	1	
1		garlic clove, minced	1	
2	tbsp.	orange juice	30	mL
3	tbsp.	lime juice	45	mL

In a medium bowl, mix all ingredients together This salsa is best when refrigerated overnight before serving.

Makes about 2 cups (500 mL) of salsa.

* If fresh papaya isn't available, substitute a 14 oz. (398 mL) can of papayas, drained and diced.

Pictured on page 109.

Mexican Meat Marinade

This is an excellent marinade for beef or pork. Marinate meat for several hours before cooking, turning occasionally. For additional flavor, baste meat frequently with marinade while grilling on barbecue.

1/4	cup	vegetable oil	60	mL
1 1/2	cups	finely chopped onion	375	mL
6		jalapeño peppers, finely chopped	6	
2		garlic cloves, minced	2	
2	tbsp.	white vinegar	30	mL
2	tbsp.	Worcestershire sauce	30	mL
14	oz.	can tomato sauce	398	mL
2	tsp.	chili powder	10	mL
1	tsp.	paprika	5	mL
1	tsp.	ground cumin	5	mL
1	tsp.	dried oregano	5	mL
1/2	tsp.	black pepper	2	mL
1/2	tsp.	cayenne pepper	2	mL

In a large saucepan, heat oil over medium-low heat; cook onions, jalapeño peppers and garlic until onions are translucent. Add all remaining ingredients; bring to a boil, cover, reduce heat and simmer for 15 minutes.

Store in refrigerator for up to 2 weeks.

Makes about 3 cups (750 mL) of marinade.

Desserts

Mangos in Kahlúa Sauce

4		ripe mangos, peeled	4	
1	cup	strawberries, washed, hulled	250	mL
1	cup	raspberries, washed	250	mL
¼	cup	sugar	60	mL
½	cup	Kahlúa	125	mL
		strawberries, for garnish		

Slice the mangos and refrigerate for at least 1 hour before serving.

Prepare the sauce by blending the strawberries, raspberries, sugar and Kahlúa in blender until very smooth.

To serve, divide the mango slices among 4 dessert plates. Pour sauce over generously and garnish with sliced strawberries.

Serves 4.

Drunken Fruit Dip

6	oz.	pkg. instant vanilla pudding	170	g
1½	cups	milk	375	mL
2	cups	whipped cream	500	mL
¼	cup	Grand Marnier	60	mL

Combine pudding with milk and beat for 2 minutes. Fold in whipped cream, then stir in Grand Marnier. Serve as a dip with a variety of fruit.

Makes about 4 cups (1 L) of dip.

Note: Whipping cream usually doubles in volume when whipped. For 2 cups (500 mL) of whipped cream, use 1 cup (250 mL) of whipping cream.

Variation: Instead of a fruit platter, try carving a fruit basket out of a watermelon. Cut off the top half of a large, whole watermelon, except for a 1½-2" (4-5 cm) strip across the center for the handle. Scoop the watermelon out of the bottom half and fill with assorted fresh fruit.

Flambéed Bananas

¼	cup	butter or margarine	60	mL
½	cup	brown sugar	125	mL
4		ripe bananas	4	
¼	cup	Kahlúa	60	mL
		vanilla ice cream		

In a chafing dish, melt butter. Add brown sugar and stir until dissolved. Slice bananas in half lengthwise; add to brown sugar mixture and stir quickly to coat. Allow to cook, stirring constantly, for approximately 1 minute. Add Kahlúa to dish and ignite with a long match. Quickly spoon flaming banana mixture over ice cream and serve.

Serves 4.

Kahlúa Cheesecake

¼	cup	melted butter or margarine	60	mL
1½	cups	chocolate wafer crumbs	375	mL
¼	tsp.	cinnamon	1	mL
4 x 8	oz.	pkgs. cream cheese, softened	4 x 250	g
1½	cups	sugar	375	mL
4		eggs	4	
1	cup	sour cream	250	mL
¼	cup	Kahlúa	60	mL
1	tsp.	vanilla	5	mL
1	cup	whipping cream	250	mL
1	cup	chocolate chips, melted	250	mL
½	tsp.	cinnamon	2	mL
8 x 1	oz.	squares semisweet chocolate	8 x 30	g
¼	cup	butter or margarine	60	mL
2	tsp.	vegetable oil	10	mL
		sweetened whipped cream, for garnish		
		cinnamon, for garnish		
12		chocolate-covered coffee beans	12	

Preheat oven to 325°F (160°C). Melt butter; add chocolate crumbs and ¼ tsp. (1 mL) cinnamon. Stir to moisten crumbs. Press evenly over bottom of a lightly greased 9" (23 cm) springform pan. Refrigerate. Beat cream cheese until smooth. Gradually add 1½ cups (375 mL) sugar; add eggs, 1 at a time, beating well after each addition. Stir in sour cream, Kahlúa, vanilla, whipping cream, melted chocolate chips and ½ tsp. (2 mL) cinnamon. Blend well.

Pour filling over chilled crust and bake for 1 hour and 15 minutes. Without opening oven door, turn heat off and leave cheesecake in oven an additional 1 hour and 15 minutes. Remove from oven and cool on wire rack for 30 minutes. Loosen rim of pan by running a knife around the edge of the cheesecake, then refrigerate at least 3 hours or overnight.

Place cheesecake on a serving plate and remove rim of pan. Melt semisweet chocolate squares, butter and vegetable oil over low heat, stirring constantly, until smooth. Spread over cheesecake, allowing glaze to drizzle down sides. Garnish with sweetened whipped cream rosettes, sprinkle rosettes lightly with cinnamon and top with a chocolate-covered coffee bean.

Serves 12.

Pictured on opposite page.

Kahlúa Cheesecake, page 126

Tropical Cheesecake

1 1/2	cups	shortbread cookie crumbs	375	mL
5	tbsp.	butter or margarine, melted	75	mL
4 x 8	oz.	pkgs. cream cheese, softened	4 x 250	g
3	cups	mashed ripe banana	750	mL
1	cup	sugar	250	mL
1/2	cup	banana liqueur	125	mL
2	tsp.	vanilla	10	mL
8		eggs	8	
1 1/2	cups	sour cream	375	mL
1	tbsp.	sugar	15	mL
1	tbsp.	banana liqueur	15	mL
1	tsp.	vanilla	5	mL
		assorted fresh fruit, for garnish		

Move oven rack to lower third of oven and preheat to 350°F (180°C). Lightly grease a 9" (23 cm) springform pan. Cut a circle of aluminum foil several inches (5-10 cm) larger than diameter of pan. In a medium bowl, combine cookie crumbs and butter. Press into bottom and partially up sides of prepared pan. Wrap outside of pan in foil. Set crust aside.

In an extra-large mixing bowl, combine cream cheese, banana, 1 cup (250 mL) sugar, 1/2 cup (125 mL) banana liqueur and 2 tsp. (10 mL) vanilla, mixing at medium speed of electric mixer until well blended. Add eggs, one at a time, mixing well after each addition. Carefully pour over crust and place springform pan in a larger shallow pan. Add enough hot water to shallow pan to bring water level 1" (2.5 cm) up sides of springform pan. Bake until the centre of the cheesecake is firm, approximately 80-90 minutes. Run a knife around the edge of the cheesecake; allow to cool completely before removing sides of pan and placing on serving dish.

In a medium mixing bowl, blend sour cream, 1 tbsp. (15 mL) sugar, 1 tbsp. (15 mL) banana liqueur and 1 tsp. (5 mL) vanilla with an electric mixer, at medium speed, until ingredients are well blended. Spread over cooled cheesecake. Cover and refrigerate overnight.

Just before serving, garnish with assorted fresh fruit such as strawberries, sliced papaya, mango, kiwi, etc., depending on market availability.

Serves 12.

Cozumel Cloud

16	oz.	pkg. Oreo cookies	500	g
1/4	cup	butter or margarine, softened	60	mL
8	oz.	cream cheese, softened	250	g
3	cups	milk	750	mL
6	oz.	pkg. instant chocolate pudding	170	g
2	cups	whipped cream	500	mL

Finely crush cookies in food processor and set aside. Cream butter and cream cheese until smooth and set aside.

In a large bowl, combine milk and pudding mix. Beat for 2 minutes, then add cream cheese mixture. Combine until smooth, then fold in whipped cream.

Line the bottom of a 2½-quart (2.5 L) glass bowl with 1/3 of the crushed cookies and top with 1/2 the chocolate mixture. Repeat, then sprinkle the remaining 1/3 of the crushed cookies on top. Refrigerate 2-3 hours before serving.

Serves 12.

Rice Pudding

1	cup	water	250	mL
1	tsp.	butter or margarine	5	mL
3/4	cup	raisins	175	mL
1	cup	uncooked instant rice	250	mL
6	oz.	pkg. instant vanilla pudding	170	g
2	cups	cereal cream	500	mL
1/2	tsp.	cinnamon	2	mL
1/4	tsp.	nutmeg	1	mL
		cinnamon, for garnish		

In a medium saucepan, bring water, butter and raisins to a boil. Stir in rice; cover, remove from heat and let stand 5 minutes.

Combine pudding mix, cream and spices and prepare as directed on pudding package.

Add rice mixture to prepared pudding, mixing well. Pour into serving dish and sprinkle with cinnamon for garnish. Chill at least 1 hour before serving.

Serves 6.

Mexican Flan

1/2	cup	brown sugar	125	mL
1	tbsp.	water	15	mL
4		eggs	4	
1 1/2	cups	water	375	mL
10 1/2	oz.	can sweetened condensed milk	300	mL
1	tsp.	vanilla	5	mL

Preheat oven to 325°F (160°C).

In a small saucepan, combine sugar and 1 tbsp. (15 mL) water. Heat over medium heat, stirring constantly, until mixture caramelizes. Pour into a 4-cup (1 L) soufflé or baking dish and swirl over bottom and about 2" (5 cm) up sides of dish.

In a medium bowl, lightly beat eggs; stir in 1 1/2 cups (375 mL) water, milk and vanilla until smooth. Pour into prepared dish. Set in a shallow pan; pour hot water into pan about 1 1/2" (4 cm) up the side of the dish.

Bake for 1 hour and 15 minutes, or until a toothpick inserted halfway between center and edge of custard comes out clean.

Leave in water bath until cooled to lukewarm, then remove from water bath, cover and refrigerate about 4 hours, or until thoroughly chilled.

Run a knife around inside edge of dish. Place a serving dish over baking dish. Hold dishes together and invert. Shake gently to release custard and lift off baking dish, allowing caramel sauce to drizzle over flan.

Serves 6.

Flan De Fresa

1½	cups	finely crushed vanilla wafers	375	mL
1/3	cup	butter or margarine, melted	75	mL
1/4	cup	sugar	60	mL
3/4	cup	pineapple-orange juice	175	mL
16	oz.	bag small marshmallows	500	g
2	cups	whipped cream	500	mL
2	cups	sliced strawberries	500	mL

Preheat oven to 375°F (190°C).

Stir together wafer crumbs, butter and sugar. Press into a 9" (23 cm) pie plate and bake for 5 minutes. Remove from oven and cool.

Heat juice; add marshmallows and stir until melted.

Chill until partially set, then fold in 1½ cups (375 mL) whipped cream and 1½ cups (375 mL) strawberries, reserving remaining whipped cream and strawberries for garnish. Pour filling into pie shell and chill.

Just before serving, garnish with remaining whipped cream and sliced strawberries.

Serves 8.

Margarita Pie

1		9" (23 cm) graham cracker crust	1	
10½	oz.	can sweetened condensed milk	300	mL
1½	oz.	tequila	45	mL
1½	oz.	Triple Sec	45	mL
4		fresh limes	4	
2-3		drops green food coloring	2-3	
1½	cups	whipped cream	375	mL
2	cups	sugar	500	mL
1	cup	cold water	250	mL
		whipped cream, for garnish		

Prepare your favorite graham crust, or use a purchased crust.

In a medium bowl, combine condensed milk, tequila and Triple Sec. Squeeze juice from all 4 limes, reserving limes for candied peel. Add lime juice and food coloring to milk mixture, then fold into whipped cream. Pour into pie shell and freeze 4-5 hours.

To serve, garnish with whipped cream and candied lime peel, (see below to make candied lime peel) if desired.

To make candied lime peel, cut off rind of limes and slice into ⅛ x 1" (3 x 25 mm) pieces. Drop into boiling water and boil, uncovered, for 10 minutes. Drain; rinse under cold water and set aside. Combine sugar and cold water in medium saucepan. Bring to a boil, stirring to dissolve sugar, then boil 5 minutes without stirring. Add lime rind and boil 15 minutes. Drain rind and let dry.

Serves 8.

Mexican Chocolate Pie

1		9" (23 cm) baked pie shell	1	
1	tbsp.	unflavored gelatin (1 envelope)	15	mL
1/2	cup	cold water	125	mL
4		eggs	4	
3 x 1	oz.	squares semisweet chocolate	3 x 30	g
2	tbsp.	sugar	30	mL
1/3	cup	Kahlúa	75	mL
1 1/2	cups	whipping cream	375	mL
2	tbsp.	sugar	30	mL
1	tsp.	vanilla	5	mL
		shaved chocolate, for garnish		

Prepare pie shell.

Sprinkle gelatin over cold water and let soften for about 5 minutes.

Separate eggs, placing 2 whites in a small bowl (refrigerate remaining 2 whites for use in another recipe) and 4 yolks in top of double boiler. Let egg whites warm to room temperature. Beat egg yolks slightly. Stir in gelatin mixture, chocolate and 2 tbsp. (30 mL) sugar. Cook over hot, not boiling, water, stirring until chocolate is melted and gelatin is dissolved, about 10 minutes.

Remove from heat, stir in Kahlua and place top of double boiler in a large bowl of ice water. Stir occasionally until cool, about 15 minutes.

In a large chilled bowl, whip cream, 2 tbsp. (30 mL) sugar and vanilla until stiff; refrigerate.

Beat the 2 room temperature egg whites until stiff peaks form. Fold egg whites and chocolate mixture into 1 1/2 cups (375 mL) whipped cream. Reserve rest of cream for garnish. Pour filling into prepared pie shell, spreading evenly. Refrigerate until firm, about 3 hours or overnight.

Garnish pie with remaining whipped cream and shaved chocolate. Keep refrigerated until ready to serve.

Serves 12.

Coca Roca Pie

1		9" (23 cm) unbaked deep-dish pie shell	1	
8		Almond Rocas, crushed	8	
1/2	cup	butter or margarine	125	mL
3 x 1	oz.	squares semisweet chocolate	3 x 30	g
3 x 1	oz.	squares unsweetened chocolate	3 x 30	g
1 1/2	cups	sugar	375	mL
3		eggs	3	
3/4	cup	flour	175	mL
8		Almond Rocas, crushed	8	
2 x 1	oz.	squares semisweet chocolate	2 x 30	g
1	tsp.	butter or margarine	5	mL
4		Almond Rocas, crushed	4	

Prepare pie shell.

Preheat oven to 350°F (180°C).

Sprinkle 8 crushed Almond Rocas over bottom of pie shell. Melt first amount of butter with semisweet chocolate and unsweetened chocolate. Add sugar, eggs and flour and beat until combined. Stir in 8 crushed Almond Rocas and pour batter into pie shell.

Bake for 50-60 minutes, or until a toothpick comes out clean.

Melt 2 squares semisweet chocolate and 1 tsp. (5 mL) butter or margarine. Spread over warm pie and sprinkle with 4 crushed Almond Rocas.

Serves 10.

Note: In total this recipe needs 20 Almond Rocas.

Kahlúa Pecan Pie

1		9" (23 cm) unbaked pie shell	1	
2	tbsp.	butter or margarine, softened	30	mL
1/2	cup	brown sugar	125	mL
2	tsp.	vanilla	10	mL
1	tbsp.	flour	15	mL
3		eggs	3	
1/2	cup	Kahlúa	125	mL
1/2	cup	dark corn syrup	125	mL
1	cup	whole pecans	250	mL

Prepare pie shell.

Preheat oven to 400°F (200°C).

Combine butter, sugar, vanilla and flour. Add eggs, 1 at a time, and continue to beat until smooth. Stir in Kahlúa and corn syrup and mix well.

Arrange pecans in bottom of unbaked pie shell and pour Kahlua mixture over top. Bake at 400°F (200°C) for 10 minutes, then reduce heat to 325°F (160°C) and bake for another 40 minutes, or until centre of pie is firm.

Serves 8.

Margarita Loaf

Loaf:

1	cup	raisins	250	mL
1/4	cup	tequila	60	mL
1/4	cup	Grand Marnier	60	mL
1/2	cup	warm water	125	mL
1	tsp.	grated lemon peel	5	mL
1	tsp.	grated lime peel	5	mL
2/3	cup	firmly packed brown sugar	150	mL
2	tbsp.	butter or margarine	30	mL
1		egg	1	
2	cups	flour	500	mL
1	tsp.	baking soda	5	mL
2/3	cup	chopped pecans	150	mL

Cheese Spread:

8	oz.	cream cheese, softened	250	g
1/4	cup	butter or margarine, softened	60	mL
2	tsp.	icing sugar	10	mL
1	tbsp.	Grand Marnier	15	mL
1	tbsp.	grated lime peel	15	mL

Preheat oven to 350°F (180°C).

In a small bowl, combine raisins, tequila, Grand Marnier, water, lemon peel and lime peel; set aside.

In a large bowl, using an electric mixer, beat sugar, butter and egg until light and fluffy.

In another bowl, combine flour and baking soda. Add to creamed mixture alternately with raisin mixture, using low to medium speed of mixer. Stir in pecans. Pour into a lightly greased 5 x 9" (13 x 23 cm) loaf pan. Bake for 50-60 minutes, or until toothpick inserted in center comes out clean. Remove from pan and cool on wire rack.

To prepare cheese spread, in a small bowl, beat cream cheese, butter and icing sugar until smooth. Stir in Grand Marnier and lime peel. Makes 1¼ cups.

To serve, slice loaf and serve with cheese spread.

Serves 8.

Index

Order Form

Light the Fire – Fiery Food with a Light New Attitude!
          _____ x 15.95 U.S (18.95 CDN)   = $_____
The Fire 'n' Ice Cookbook – Mexican Food with a Bold New Attitude
          _____ x 14.95 U.S (16.95 CDN)   = $_____
Pure Ground Medium Red Chile Powder - 2 oz. package
          _____ x 4.95 U.S (5.95 CDN)   = $_____
Pure Ground Medium Red Chipotle Chile Powder - 2 oz. package
          _____ x 6.95 U.S (8.95 CDN)   = $_____

Shipping:
  $4.00 for the first book (or book equivalent) and
  $2.00 for each additional book (or book equivalent)
  - There is no additional charge for shipping spices
  when ordered with books   = $_____
                              Subtotal   = $_____
  Sales tax in Canada add applicable GST (7%)   = $_____
                              Total order   = $_____

Payment: O Check or   Credit card: O AMEX or O VISA

Card number: _____   Expiry date: _____ / _____

Name on card: _____

U.S. and international orders are payable in U.S. funds.

Name:_____

Street:_____

City: _____   Prov./State_____

Country: _____   Postal Code/Zip:_____

For fund raising or volume purchases, contact
MJM Grande Enterprises Ltd. for volume discount rates.